The Great American Deer Camp

NORTH★AMERICAN★HUNTING★CLUB

The Great American Deer Camp

Bryce Towsley
Jim Casada
John Barsness
Lance Krueger
Ron Bahls
Tom Fegely
Jim Van Norman
Tom Carpenter

EDITED BY
Tom Carpenter

North American Hunting Club
Minnetonka, Minnesota

The Great American Deer Camp

Mike Vail
Vice President, Product Marketing/Business Development

Tom Carpenter
Director of Book and New Media Development

Dan Kennedy
Book Production Manager

Heather Koshiol
Book Development Coordinator

Zachary Marell
Book Design and Production

ISBN: 1-58159-070-9

1 2 3 4 5 6 / 02 01 00 99

North American Hunting Club
12301 Whitewater Drive
Minnetonka, MN 55343

Photo Credits

Cover onlay (clockwise from left): Bryce Towsley
(2, top), Lance Krueger, John Barsness

All other photos copyright © individual authors
except: Phil Aarrestad, 129, 130, 131 (bottom), 178;
John Barsness, 3 (2, top), 5; Tom Carpenter, 115,
126 (top), 127, 131 (left), 133, 170, 175, 190 (right);
Eileen Clarke, 58, 72 (large photo), 73; Betty Lou
Fegely, 3; Tom and Betty Lou Fegely, 140–169; John
Ford, 223; Donald M. Jones, 63; Lance Krueger, 3
(top), 4; Bob McNally, 37, 38, 46, 47 (top), 50 (top),
51 (bottom), 54 (bottom), 55 (bottom right); Greg
Schwieters, 28, 117, 119, 195, 196, 206 (both), 209;
Keith Sutton, 36, 38, 40, 41 (both), 48 (both), 49;
Bryce Towsley, 2 (2, bottom), 6 (top), 7; John J.
Woods, 50 (2, bottom), 54 (top), 55 (top), 57.

CONTENTS

Introduction

EXPLORING THE
GREAT AMERICAN DEER CAMP

Someone who doesn't hunt deer might be surprised at what they find in this book. Sure, there are tales of hunting adventures, pictures of deer in fields and forests, photos of deer being held by successful hunters, and images of cabins and tents and trailers and other accommodations one might live in while hunting deer somewhere in North America.

But there's much more.

A hunter—someone who has gone to sleep to the hiss and crackle of a woodstove, sat around a campfire with friends or family the evening before Opening Day, slept in a tent with a million stars all around and then rose before dawn to hunt, walked the long trail back to camp in a golden sunset—now that's a person who knows what deer camp is really about and wouldn't be at all surprised at what is in this book.

It's obvious, from the eight stories to come, that deer camp is about much more than just hunting, or how many deer hang from the meatpole. Each of these stories hits on some combination of aspects ...

Traditions. History. The Land. Change. Family. Friends. Relationships. Special people gone to a better hunting ground. Struggles against the elements as well as ourselves. Escape. Good Food. Stories. Laughter. Death. Life.

Yet there is also a common thread that's more subtle, and you'll sense it in the words of each author as well as the pictures they've brought you: that deer camp is special, a time and place and state-of-mind that we long for and need, not just for the hunting, but for the feelings it creates in us ... feelings that live within all year 'round.

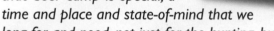

So let's explore. From a wall tent at Montana timberline to a hunt with dogs in the swamps of South Carolina. From a row of trailers in the Texas brush to a lodge in Pennsylvania's Poconos. From a house on the edge of a Wisconsin farmtown to a knot of cabins a hundred miles out on the Wyoming prairie. And from a converted barn in the flat forests of northern Minnesota to a tarpaper-and-plastic shack hidden in the Vermont mountains.

You'll see that, in the end, it doesn't really matter where deer camp is, or what it is, or even how you go about conducting it. The search for deer camp's real meaning—and it's likely a little different for each of us—is good. Probably, most of us never really want to find that meaning, but just keep coming back to look for it year after year—living, breathing, being there and just being able to say yes, I was at deer camp this year. And that in itself makes deer camp worthwhile and important.

Come on a journey through The Great American Deer Camp.

New England Woods

Vermont

Vermont Deer Camps: An Evolution

The deer hunting tradition is strong in New England, and deer camp's roots run deep. Yes, this region was among the first settled in our country, centuries ago. But much of the land is still wild—wilder than you would think, often second- or even third-growth timber as nature continues to reclaim its hold—and deer camps abound.

BRYCE TOWLSEY explores them here, but digs even deeper into the changing face of the Vermont deer camp. He searches for the answer: Will the children of New England grow into adulthood yearning for deer camp like their fathers, and their fathers before them? If so, will it be the same deer camp, or a new deer camp?

This is his search for the answers, along with a look into some Vermont deer camps of both yesterday and today.

Vermont Deer Camps: An Evolution
By Bryce Towsley

As deer hunters we all spend a lot of time in stands, and I suppose it's human nature to gravitate to those we like best. One of mine is a split maple tree halfway up a bottleneck created by the north-facing ledges on a mountain deep in the heart of Vermont's Taconic Range. It was here, almost by accident, that I took my first archery deer, mixed up somewhere in the middle of missing more whitetails than I would choose to remember. During the many hours in my early years of bowhunting spent in that stand, I learned much about frustration. But with that singular doe I also learned about elation, and that a little of it can wipe out a lot of frustration.

Another favorite, a stand that produced five bucks in as many years, is in a hemlock tree a mile from my house. Yet one more is a shaky permanent stand clinging to a tired oak tree high on a ridgetop an hour's drive away. That one has never produced a deer for me, but sure has given me a bunch of October memories.

Even now, after hunting from hundreds of stands across North America, those from my early years remain special; I expect they will until I am in the grave. But they are not my favorite. The place with the best memories was a perch on the steep stairway that leads to the sleeping loft of our family deer camp. It was here that my strongest and most enduring deer hunting memories were formed.

Back in the Pleistocene era of the 1960s, before enlightenment brought its many changes, Vermont deer camps were a man's domain: No ladies, no babies and no apologies. This was a masculine world filled with a smoky haze, hard drinks, high testosterone, harsh language and rough jokes. It was a place where a man could cut loose, revert to a hairier time and act as all men

The ladder to the Camp Buckless sleeping loft offers more than just a route to rest. Here, another generation discovers that the perch is just right for listening to deer camp tales.

must from time to time. I longed to be a part of it so much I thought I would burst.

But to my eternal anguish, the rule at "Camp Buckless" was that to spend the night you must be at least 16 years old. There was a little bending and I was allowed day visits at 12. I used the time to lobby hard for the rules to be further relaxed. I don't know how many floors I swept or how many times I loaded the wood stove, but with some coaxing from my Uncle Butch the long-standing rule was waived for me, the first of my generation, and I started to hunt there in my thirteenth year.

It has been more than 30 years, but I remember every detail, how in awe of it all I was. I remember how I sat concentrating hard so that I could remember everything.

Even today I can still recall the smell of the camp, a unique scent that I could identify blindfolded. I can remember sitting perched on that ladder (for it's much too steep to be realistically called stairs) and looking down at this group of

men that I knew so well, yet who now seemed so strange. I remember listening carefully to my grandfather and the others telling stories of the glories of past hunts and rough jokes—which my young mind understood only in knowing somehow that by hearing them, I had taken the first step to being accepted as one of the men.

I recall the strange and powerful longing that was threatening to devour my guts, a longing to belong to this group, to fit in. I knew that my invited presence was a sign that I was on the road to that acceptance, but didn't really have a clue how I could tell when I finally got there.

Even when I am old and my life's behind me, it will still be fresh in my mind how I reveled in that first weekend in camp and how I tried so hard to please, to fit in, to be one of the guys—all the while knowing in my heart that I was failing. I can still feel the anxiety and the terrorizing knowledge that I would never get it right. How could I know that only time could make it work? I was 13; what did I know about time?

No matter what generation the participants belong to, deer camp is a place to learn: about rifles and cartridges and hunting topics of all kinds, of course. But it's also where many boys (and girls, more and more these days) first learn to become adults.

In deer camp, even the most mundane of tasks takes on meaning—just feeling good and being there makes everything easy.

I remember so well the excitement of that first night and how the camp seemed to have a life of its own, one fed by the power of these men, a power too strong to be contained. In my youth, I could sense it—but it puzzled me. It was, I now understand, the power of anticipation. An anticipation that only can be generated in the waning hours before the deer season opened. That anticipation fueled an excitement that permeated the camp until it filled any and all available space, overwhelming everybody there, and I knew that no one in that room would ever again have friends as good or as close as those who were with them at the moment.

Good times (at deer camp they're almost all good times) from the author's early years at Camp Buckless, including a bear who met his maker on the mountain behind camp.

An earlier time, but deer camp's elements are ageless: good food, good coffee, laughter, warm sleeping bags, oil lamps ... and the never-ending hope that tomorrow will bring a buck across your path.

I can still taste the huge "grownup" breakfast my Uncle Bud cooked the next morning and the bitterness of the coffee as it scalded my taste buds for the first time in my young life. Old injuries and years of shooting have ruined my eardrums, but even today I can clearly hear the squeak of the snow as we left the camp in the dark, and I remember vividly the stark contrast of the cold and clean northern air to the camp's humid and smoky interior.

It's so easy for me to venture back to that morning on the edge of the hardwoods as I sat with my back against a big maple tree, shivering but not entirely from the cold. I can feel the cold steel and the dark stained wood of the old Winchester that Gramp had loaned to me amid solemn vows and sworn oaths to treat it like it was the most delicate treasure on earth, because in my mind it truly was. I can smell my father's unfiltered Pall Malls mixing with the sharp chemical odor rising from my own freshly dry-cleaned wool coat and see the cigarette's glow as he smoked beside me in the dark.

There have been so many days of deer hunting in the years between that one and today, and most have faded from memory. But that day remains as vivid as it was in 1968.

I remember how boredom replaced excitement as the day played out, but that it didn't seem to matter. I also recall how things that are now vexing or at least mundane were pure excitement, and how the newness of all the experiences threatened to overwhelm me.

The camp was deep in the woods at the end of miles of bad road, a road rutted deep with mud and mined with ledges and hidden boulders. That night we hit one that hung the snow-plow frame on the old Jeep and in spite of chains on all wheels, we were stuck. To the others in the truck it was a reason for more bad language and foul tempers, but for me it was grand adventure.

Later as we pulled into the camp yard, the dim, mud-crusted headlights swept quickly across a bear that was hanging from the meat pole. It was the first bear I could recall seeing and that quick glimpse scared me breathless. But at the same time, deep down, it excited me. It was true! There were bears lurking in these woods we were hunting! The element of danger, adventure and excitement stirred by that knowledge generated in my young soul a thirst for it all that was beyond measure and unquenchable even today.

That evening, as I sat in my "stand" listening to the story of the bear, I barely dared to breathe, afraid I might miss a syllable. In the following weeks and years I spent many happy hours perched halfway up that ladder, and I am sure that it was pivotal in my life's direction. Those early days at deer camp undoubtedly helped lay the foundation for my lifelong interest in shooting and hunting, an interest that would evolve into my livelihood and in truth, my life. Perched on that ladder I felt like I was part of something big, something strange, exotic, mystifying and oh, so desirable. I felt like a member of this glorious deer-hunting fraternity.

From that day and for many years all my deer hunting revolved around deer camps. There was a time when I couldn't imagine there was anything else, and my most enduring memories have grown out of that association.

It was only a year or so later and not too far from the camp when my Uncle Butch shot a bear that taught him a lesson about rifles, shot placement and good luck. In those days Butch (and most every one else I knew) was shooting a lever action rifle and a 19th century cartridge. His was an old Marlin Model 1893 chambered in .38-55 Winchester. Butch was young and quick and when most hunters would have done little more than watch the running bear, Butch snapped off a shot with a blinding speed that later would save him. Leads are hard to figure with those pokey old cartridges, and his first bullet hit the bear a bit too far back. The liver hit would certainly have been fatal, but another trait of those old cartridges was that while they effectively killed the game by punching big holes in them, unlike modern cartridges they transferred very little shock, so it sometimes took a while for the critter to figure out he was dead.

The question has been raised many times since if the bear charged, or in his confusion simply picked Butch's direction to run, but he let out a roar and came right at him. (For what it's worth, Butch was the only one other than the bear who was there and he says he thinks the bear was charging. The bear isn't saying.) Butch fired fast, the lever a blur as he fed cartridge after cartridge into the chamber, but still the bear kept coming. Finally, the last bullet in the gun hit the bear between the eyes and Butch had to jump out of the way to avoid being run over as it skidded past him.

The odd thing is that he usually loaded the tube magazine, worked the action to chamber a shell and went hunting. But for some inexplicable reason that morning he had put another shell in the magazine, replacing the one he had chambered. That was the shot that killed the bear. Oh yeah, he bought a pump action .270 Winchester the next week.

This fueled my young mind with more terror and excitement, and for a long time after, every sound I heard in the woods was made by a giant bear intent on having me as *hors d'oeuvres*. I was hunting then with an old Winchester Model 1892 in .38-40 Winchester that Gramp had loaned me. As I recall it held some-

The stories—of deer and bear and big adventures and close calls—all happen outside, but the tales live on within the walls of deer camp. Heading in after a day on the mountain: What tales will come through the door with the hunter?

thing like 14 shots and I always had it loaded full, with extras within easy reach in my pockets. Maybe a bear would get me, but he'd have to work at it because I didn't intend to go without a fight.

There was another morning when the deer were everywhere and even my father (who loved deer camp, but wasn't often a successful hunter) shot a buck. It was a feast of adventure to this young hunter and while I didn't even see a deer that morning, I couldn't have been more excited as

we loaded venison into Dad's old Jeep station wagon until the springs flattened.

I shot my first buck back there in that same location, a place we had named "the pantry." (If you were at camp and wanted some deer meat, you went to the "pantry" to get it.) I was in a treestand built by Butch who, in addition to a new phobia of bears, was deathly afraid of heights. The stand was only 5 feet off the ground and was a log platform so large you could hold a square dance on it. I sat perched there early one cold and silent morning when a spike-horn buck

When you're young and at deer camp, it's all an adventure ... and sometimes a lesson in determination and growing up, waiting there in the cold to try and shoot your first deer.

came running past. One shot from the .243 I had handled thousands of hay bales one summer to buy, and I was the most excited hunter at camp for the rest of the season.

The years passed quickly and with them the memories changed, but never the excitement. Everywhere else, I was made to grow up. But at deer camp I'll always be 13.

Deer season has remained the most magic time of the year and the Friday night before the season opens is when the excitement peaks. One year a quest to burn off some of the energy evolved into an arm wrestling match. I was in my twenties and, after a few years in a telephone company line crew, as strong as I would ever be. I challenged all takers and lost only once, late in the evening when I was sore and fatigued. My pride was little compensation, though, when for the first three days of the hunting season I couldn't raise my arm enough to shoot a rifle and the whitetails were in little danger.

I had met the woman who would become my wife and like any man whose little girl is dating, her dad didn't seem to like me much. I knew he liked to hunt, so I invited him to camp one day, hoping to open the door a crack, so to speak.

We drove in early in the morning looking for a cup of coffee before setting off to hunt. The first out of bed to greet us was a regular who hadn't hunted for years. He was there for the camp life, not the deer hunting, and he left no doubt about that: While he played by the rules all year, at camp he made his own rules. I think because it was as much an act of defiance against society's restraints as anything else, he started every morning with a few shots of Black Velvet whiskey. I guess he was just being polite when, rather than coffee, he offered us whiskey. We declined, as he knew we would, and I put the coffee on to perk, not thinking anything more of it. That night we returned to the camp for dinner. For reasons nobody can remember we have always called the backstrap of a deer the "woodchuck," so nobody thought much about it when Bud said that he had put a whole "woodchuck" in the stew we were eating.

The next day I got a call. "My father's upset. He said that you guys drink whiskey for breakfast and eat rodents for dinner. He thinks that maybe I ought to look around a little more!"

It was later when I was deep in the woods and far from camp before I realized I had left my lunch on the table. I used my '06 to shoot the head off a snowshoe hare and built a fire to cook him for lunch. I had

> *I shot my first buck back there in ... a place we had named "the pantry." (If you were at camp and wanted some deer meat, you went to the "pantry" to get it.)*

Checking the tracks, northern Vermont. Was it a buck? Where is he now? The hunt continues.

invited my father-in-law-to-be back to the camp that weekend, hoping to repair some of the damage done by the first trip. He was hunting the same area as I, had heard the shot and wandered by to see if anybody needed help dragging a buck. We sat by the fire most of the afternoon cooking the rabbit, which turned out so tough it was barely edible. But it didn't matter. We bonded a friendship that endures even today.

Five years after that, I was ready to quit hunting. It had been a tough year, my mother dying in February at the age of 48, then six weeks later my grandfather passing away as well. He was the closest thing I had to a mentor, and deer hunting was the glue that bonded our lives. On this opening morning it would have been impossible not to be thinking about him. I was lost, confused and mad at a world I didn't understand. I cared little for anything, and most of all I had decided I cared nothing about deer hunting. I left the camp anyway that opening morning and walked to an old logging road where I stood for a long time in the falling snow, my mind drifting.

I had decided to return to camp, pack my things and go home when something told me to walk up the logging road a little further. I knew it was Gramp and so I did. Suddenly a noise unlike any I have heard before or since caused me to freeze. Then I heard it again. It was a deer snorting, but unlike any deer I had heard snort before or since. I knew it was a deer because it was running right at me. The doe passed by at 20 feet with a small buck right behind her. I watched, not sure what to do next, when a movement caught my eye and I saw the rack on the next deer. The buck caught the movement of my rifle and stopped for an instant. I shot and he ran into the swamp. The track was short and I dressed the deer, cleaned the blood off my hands and knife in the snow and then sat down beside the animal.

For a long time I sat, not really thinking about anything, just drifting again. In a while I realized I would never give up hunting, but it was the last time I ever hunted from that camp.

There have been many camps in the intervening years—some as simple and rustic as some plastic nailed on a few trees, some so fancy that champagne and caviar were on the menu. Each has imprinted on me its own unique memories.

The Plastic Camp is where I learned to bowhunt and where that first-mentioned tree-stand remains today, surrounded by other trees with broadheads buried in them. Rustic beyond belief, that camp was simply some sheets of plastic mated with bits of scrap lumber and nailed around a few trees. Its best feature was a dry tin roof supported by a rough collection of branches and scrap lumber. The floor was dirt and because the bedrock was only inches below the

At "The Plastic Camp"—rustic beyond belief but filled with hundreds of happy memories and tales.

surface, it was hard and not at all level enough for a good night's sleep.

The camp belonged to a friend of Butch's who invited us to try our hand on the deer there, and somehow the rustic nature added to its appeal. The dirt floor raised enough dust to leave us filthy within hours, and the thin plastic walls had us freezing with the stove glowing red. But I loved the place anyway.

A big hickory tree served as one corner-post. The nuts on this tree were huge, heavy and as solid as kryptonite. Sometimes late at night when the wind was blowing and I lay sleeping on the top bunk they would drop on the metal roof, just inches from my face. The noise would, as they say, "wake the dead" and would scare me nearly enough to join them. I would lie there the rest

of the night listening to the wind and waiting for the next nut to drop. If it did or didn't was irrelevant; sleep would not be visiting again. As if that wasn't enough, the bed itself was so tilted that if I did drift off, I would find myself piled up in my sleeping bag at the foot several times a night.

In the darkness we were invaded by raccoons, skunks and porcupines, while daylight would have chipmunks and squirrels tearing up the place. One of my buddies was terrified of the porcupines and worried that one would climb into bed with him as he slept. He would shoot every one that showed up and more than once we had to scour the ground outside for arrows so he could hunt in the morning. Those arrows' passage from inside the camp did little to ensure the integrity of the plastic walls, and duct tape

was certain I was dying. I staggered out the door, running only on instinct, and tripped over somebody collapsed on the ground outside.

When the clear air re-took our lungs, we looked back into the camp and saw smoke and fire shooting two feet out of the top of the stove. (I think it was about then that we gave up on any thoughts of keeping our camo "scent free.")

Being sheet metal, the stove had little weight and when the wood inside shifted it hit the side, knocking the stove off the rock and pulling the smoke pipe off. We fixed the problem, but I laid wide-eyed on my bunk and never slept a wink until I was in my treestand, which later collapsed, but that's another story.

Each year on the evening before the archery season opened we would eat huge steaks, cooked by the camp owner over an open oak-wood fire, and we would toast all things good in the world with a bottle of cheap wine. We would tell jokes, harass each other and know that while we would try, no one would sleep that night even if the stove behaved.

That hardwood ridge with its drafty camp tucked into a hollow was a magical place and I miss hunting there, but time changes all things and we must move on. Only memories can remain. It was there, though, that I reaffirmed the knowledge that there is no experience in this world that can match being in deer camp with good friends on the night before the season opens.

It had been a few years since I had hunted from a camp so I was excited when one year my cousin decided in mid-summer to build a camp on the mountain behind his house. Time was a struggle, but by the time the November rifle deer season opened we had a camp built and the fire-

became as crucial as oxygen. My buddy didn't like skunks much either, but we drew a line there. Safe passage seemed the best strategy, so we hid his arrows.

Because of the uneven floor, some creative engineering was needed for anything that was brought in or built. We thought we were clever when we leveled the sheet-metal stove using a rock under one leg until sometime in the night I woke to a world encased in a dense, red fog. I couldn't see, I couldn't breathe, my lungs were screaming for air, my head was pounding and I

Deer season is cold in Vermont, and a good heat source is a necessity. This barrel stove (opposite) is a little steadier on its feet than the one in the accompanying tale.

wood cut. A few weeks before opening day I took my kids to see it and to do a little scouting.

My five-year-old girl didn't like the mile-long four-wheeler ride as much as my little boy, but they both loved the camp. Walking in the woods with Dad, while not exactly a silent experience, was educational for them. They picked up acorns until their pockets bulged and looked for deer tracks. I showed them their first scrape. We found some saplings that a buck had rubbed on and we checked out some "other" deer sign. At two (and a half, as he was quick to remind me) years of age, my boy found tracks by himself and identified them as "a big buck." They looked like a fawn to me, but who was I to argue?

We ate lunch at the camp and played a game of cards. While they climbed on the beds and pretended to be sleeping I sat and watched them and wondered if in a few years they would be staying here with me, buzzing with the excitement and anticipation of opening day. Will deer hunting be as important to them as it is to me and will I even be able to convey that importance to them when the time is right?

Will they someday come to feel the magic of the first morning? Will I be teacher enough to show them that deer hunting is so much more than just shooting an animal? Will I be able to share the excitement of dawn sneaking into the woods or the sadness as darkness overtakes the day at the end? Can I explain the emotions the smell of Vermont's mountains and northwoods in late fall can stir in my soul? Will my children sit in this camp in wonderment of all the new and exciting experiences? Will they, as I have come to, associate the sounds, the smells, the "feelings" of a camp with good thoughts, with happy memories?

I think my destiny has always been written and, even without that first deer camp deep in the Green Mountains, I am certain that I would still be a deer hunter, but I question if it would continue to burn so deeply in my soul. Without that camp to indoctrinate me to the ritualistic social aspects of deer hunting, wouldn't it all be diminished? If I were to have become simply a deer hunter and not part of that deer-camp fraternity, would not my perspective have changed?

I sometimes wonder if we, as deer hunters, are losing our way. Is this new competitive drive to shoot bigger bucks—the quest for the almighty Boone and Crockett Club score—a result, at least in part, of too many people who have emerged as deer hunters without hunting camps? Have we abandoned the essence of deer hunting and with it those intangible things that created its magic for generations? Have we collectively sold our souls in return for higher scores? Are losing the traditions founded in family deer camps the price we have paid? Who can really say? But I know that the reasons for deer hunting seemed a lot clearer when hunting from deer camps was more prevalent, when mentors, rather than videos, taught us how it was done and when a buck was a buck and any one was a good one.

The question that nags me most is: Are we really ready to abandon those sacred traditions?

Or is it me who has been wandering and has turned my back on deer-camp traditions? Have I become blinded by the opportunities that have been afforded me in the whitetail world and forgotten my roots? These questions troubled me as my children, now older, become hunters and are looking to me to show them the way.

I decided to see, to look again at Vermont's camps, to find out if the essence is still there or if it too has been sold out to the gods of big bucks (of both the dollar and the animal kind) and video games. It might be poetic that to free my time for the short Vermont gun season required that I cancel a planned hunt in Saskatchewan. Since Milo Hanson took his world-record whitetail buck in that western Canadian province, it has become Mecca for serious deer hunters—the holy land, a shrine that must be visited by all true believers. A decision to forgo a hunt there to wander the Vermont woods—where a realistic chance at any buck, let alone a trophy, is as scarce as a perfect day—was looked at by many as proof that I was completely and irreversibly insane.

At first I took this attitude as another symptom of what's gone wrong with deer hunting, but then, when the hunting was tough and the bucks scarce, for a while even I believed they could be right. But in the end, even though I failed to take a buck in Vermont that year, I found something better. I found a renewed faith in deer hunting. I found that while the traditions of Vermont

The search—for deer, for other answers—continues. Vermont's Northeast Kingdom.

I think my destiny has always been written and, even without that first deer camp deep in the Green Mountains, I am certain that I would still be a deer hunter ...

deer camps have changed, they are still with us and in some ways are improved. In searching, I could see that while we may have wandered off into the wilderness a bit, we have not forsaken deer camp's roots. The Vermont deer camp, while scarcer and certainly different, is still alive and well.

While the rough-and-tumble camps of my youth no doubt remain, for the most part the face of the Vermont deer camp has changed rather dramatically. We now have a kinder and gentler deer camp, a deer camp where children are often welcome and those youngsters are just as likely to be girls as they are boys. I found that where American society has become more tolerant and expectant of rough language, many deer camps have moved in the other direction. Gone are the crude jokes and four letter vocabularies, replaced with a respect and understanding that it's no longer just a man's world. Smoking is banned inside most camps, a sacrifice to scent-free hunting more than political correctness, and hard drinking has evolved to a polite cocktail before dinner or no alcohol at all.

But what of the focus, deer hunting?

The hunting has grown more serious. The white-tail boom has definitely found its way into our northwoods camps. A fly on the wall listening to the quiet, late night conversations will find the topics have changed. Today they will likely tune in to talk of scrape lines, rutting behavior, scent control or the current moon phase ... topics that probably would have been laughed at in our grandfather's camps.

The old traditional plaid wool jackets and pants are still around, but they are seen more with the graybeards in camp. The younger hunters will more often be wearing the latest camo patterns coupled with Gore-Tex, Thinsulate or some other high-tech material.

The old .30-30 Winchester Model 94 lever action that once dominated these woods is hardly seen today. More likely the gun rack will be filled with stainless steel bolt-action rifles with synthetic stocks and chambered for a hot, high-velocity cartridge loaded with the newest technologically advanced wonder-bullet. Gramp's peep sight is gone too, replaced with multi-coated, variable-power scopes clear enough to peer into last week.

We now see hand-held GPS satellite navigation units and laser range finders, but even with these aids, hunters no longer simply leave the camp and wander the mountains all day. Four wheelers have replaced shoe leather to reach the top of the mountains. And portable treestands rule the day.

In Gramp's day it was a badge of honor to be the man who had gone the longest in camp without a shower. Today there are scent-controlling soaps, special bags to store your clothing in and cover scents to hide what's left. And the thought of paying $10 for an ounce of animal urine would have been howled at in the old days; today we consider it a bargain.

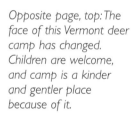

Opposite page, top: The face of this Vermont deer camp has changed. Children are welcome, and camp is a kinder and gentler place because of it.

Right: The hunting has changed over time too, going more high-tech not only on the caliber and choice of rifles, but also in clothing, scent control, optics, GPS units, rangefinders and so forth. Yet they still got deer "way back when" too— lots of them—before all this gadgetry.

Even the times when the camps are used have changed. In years past these camps laid dormant for months on end. They might see an occasional snowmobiling weekend or a little pre-season scouting/bird hunting occupancy, but the main show centered on the traditionally short Vermont rifle deer season. For as long as anybody alive can remember it's been 16 days in November, starting two Saturdays before Thanksgiving and concluding on the Sunday following that holiday. When compared to the other 50 weeks of the year, that's a painfully short time.

Traditionally, deer season was a time when anybody worthy of the name "deer hunter" was spending his days in the woods and his nights at camp. Those who could took a week off and a very lucky few managed to spend the entire deer season away from the realities of the workplace. The remainder of us struggled through the work week and arrived Friday night at the camp's door ready to forget the world until Monday morning.

For all though, it was a frenzied and sacred time. Each hunter recognized that three weekends or even 16 days out of a year is far too little for something you truly loved. So hunters attacked the deer season with an abandon that swelled these camps to near bursting, while the rest of the year they sat vacant and waiting.

Then the whitetail boom brought its changes. Today the camp occupants are just as likely to be hunting with a bow or blackpowder gun. Archery hunting exploded with the advent of compound bows, extended seasons and bag limits that now allow several deer in multiple seasons. Following that came the mini-boom that grew in a similar manner with muzzleloader hunters. As state after state, including Vermont, introduced special blackpowder seasons and the gun companies made rifles that looked more like our familiar and comfortable deer rifles, hunters embraced blackpowder as they had archery only a few years before.

The main event still remains the regular gun season, but the pace is less frantic, the drive less frenzied now. With several weeks of archery or blackpowder hunting on either end of the rifle season, the urgency is reduced. Today we can get a complete whitetail hunting fix over a few months and not risk a two-week overload.

This has made for some subtle changes in the camps' use structure and likely was a catalyst for the social changes that are so evident. Perhaps this relaxing has allowed a change from those frenzied, testosterone-fueled few days that passed by so fast each year. Now there is more time, less urgency, more weekends and less need to run on the ragged edge.

Below: It's dormant now, but for two weeks a year it becomes the center of the universe for a group of Vermont hunters. And more and more these days, with archery and muzzleloader seasons and the like, it will see use beyond that traditional November rifle season.

Above: Fifty years ago, a rifle line-up like this would have featured lever-action .30 30s, maybe a sporterized Springfield or two. Today, the story is very different.

No doubt, too, the changes have been influenced by us baby boomers and our own kids who are growing up. Even though modern times are a busier time for everybody, parents (particularly fathers) are more involved with their children. We see deer season less as a time to escape the world, including wives and kids, and more as a time to involve the family in something that's important to us.

But an ominous storm is looming on the horizon for Vermont deer hunters. I could see the indications at each of the camps I visited. Vermont is a changing state and our rural traditions are in peril. Private land ownership and land use, both public and private, are under attack and our side—that of regular, everyday people who just want to hunt—is losing.

In returning to "Camp Buckless," two things jumped out at me. First was that my own kids, particularly my 10-year-old son Nathan, were drawn to the same ladder and it quickly became his "stand" of choice. The second was the changes in the land. The first miles of the road leading in are lined with houses and the

Deep thought. Are they sharing the same concerns as their father, who writes about the storm on the horizon for Vermont deer hunters? Or are they just tired from tramping around the mountain, scouting for deer and hoping to get a shot at a grouse?

Photographs document the members and memories of this Vermont deer camp. In what form will the tradition live on?

last with camps. Because the land "Camp Buckless" is on borders a national forest, it remains the last stop for any vehicle traveling the road, or at least those able to navigate the still "unimproved" road. But just before the camp comes into sight a new road, although a gated one, breaks to the right. It loops around the camp to join the primary road that continues unmaintained past the camp, a few hundred yards beyond the property. That road, which was always nothing more than a washed out foot path over the mountains, is now groomed, fitted with water bars and marked with so many signs that no one could get lost.

In places where the years have eroded the old road bed to rocks and deep ravines it has been rerouted. I once had a stand in a forgotten apple orchard, near where I shot that last buck. I spent many November nights shivering in that big pine

tree watching the deer that traveled through and it was there that my friend with porcupine-phobia shot a bear with his bow. The bruin ran to the nearby beaver pond and died in the middle. A cold, naked swim in the icy waters was necessary to recover him.

Now the road runs right under the stand and so many people are using it that I wouldn't think of shedding my clothes. I learned that the Forest Service built it for hikers, horseback riders and snowmobiles to travel. Most don't hunt, many don't approve of hunting and some of its travelers even believe they have a divine right to stop us from hunting. The reason the government built a loop around the camp is in part because of vandalism in hunting camps. I can't help but wonder how much of that vandalism is perpetrated by sanctimonious crusaders in the name of "animal rights?"

Of course, once you leave the road there are still miles of woods to roam—most of it unseen by today's "wilderness travelers," but somehow it's all changed.

Paul Thomas used to come to our camp and when he decided to build one of his own, he chose a location a few miles away. His is a nice camp—warm, well-designed and soundly built. It's occupied by people who know how to have fun, and it's the kind of camp where memories are created. It is first and foremost a hunting camp, populated by serious whitetail hunters and the guys there were quick to tell me that the hunting is best where the land has been logged.

"Without logging we would be wasting our time," Paul's son Matt told me. "It keeps the land regenerating and provides new growth for deer habitat. If you travel off the roads and deep into the woods where it hasn't been logged in many years, the woods are sterile and empty. Mature forest is just not good wildlife habitat."

They hunt primarily in the state and national forest, so they thought they would be relatively unaffected by the new Vermont law regulating logging on private land. But in recent years the environmentalists have tied up a large portion of the logging contracts in the national forest through litigation. More recently they stopped all logging completely by finding (under circumstances that many find suspicious) an endangered Indiana bat. No matter that it was miles from Paul's camp as well as most other locations in the national forest; as I write this all logging has been suspended in the national forest in the state of Vermont.

As the power of the extreme environmentalists grows in Vermont, they are within sight of some of their goals: no logging in the national forest, no new roads and the closing of existing roads. The land the people from Paul's camp, "Camp Buckless" and thousands of other Vermont deer camps hunt on may well become an inaccessible wasteland in the name of the new "environmentalism."

Scenes from Paul Thomas's camp. Left: The main living area. Above: A blast of heat feels real good at the end of the day. Right: The faces say it all: There's nowhere else we'd rather be.

The Mason farm is in Pawlet, Vermont, which is the town that has year after year led the state in total deer kill. While not exactly a deer camp in the true sense of the definition, their large family uses the home of their parents as a "deer camp" of sorts. It's the gathering place during the hunting season, a warm haven on a cold day and a place where you can be sure that you will leave with your belly full of something good.

I have been privileged to have an invitation to hunt there through my friendship with Bryan Mason, and it was because of his and his brother Keith's efforts that both of my kids took their first whitetail deer this year. Kids are a big part of hunting here, and you only have to visit this farm during Vermont's one-day youth deer season—or any other deer season for that matter—to see that

the Masons believe in giving something back to the sport and in helping the next generation of hunters build their own traditions.

But it may not last. Like so many other farms in the state, economic changes have ensured that it's no longer viable as a working dairy farm. On top of that, rising land values and out-of-control government budgets have increased the property taxes until they are becoming a large burden. New laws founded in socialism—such as Vermont's controversial Act 60, which among other things implements a state property tax with a class structure, placing a higher assessment on plots of land larger than a 2-acre "homestead"— have laid the groundwork to guarantee that property taxes will only continue to rise. New land-use regulations have made it difficult to generate

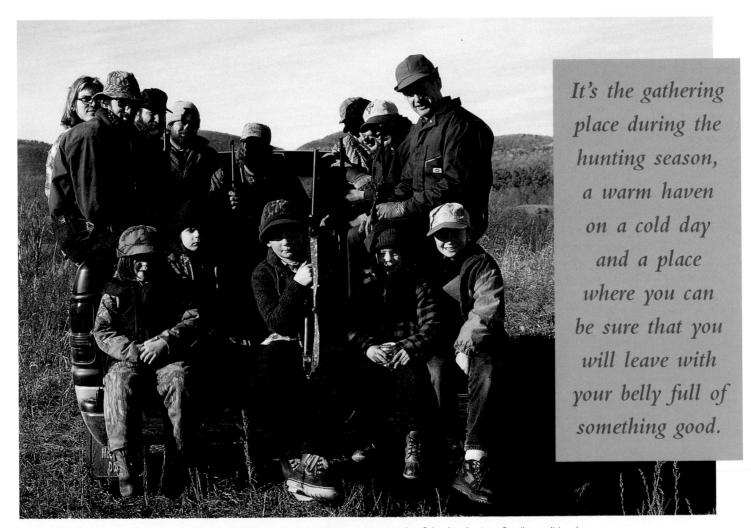

It's the gathering place during the hunting season, a warm haven on a cold day and a place where you can be sure that you will leave with your belly full of something good.

On the Mason Farm, Pawlet, Vermont. Hunting—and being good stewards of the land—is a family tradition here.

Left: Lunchtime on the Mason farm. Below (two photos): First buck, shot on the Mason farm, and the long drag out.

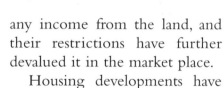

any income from the land, and their restrictions have further devalued it in the market place.

Housing developments have intruded along the edges and posted signs are becoming all too common. Many of the people moving in are hostile to hunting and active in government. It will take a big effort for this land to remain in the family and open to hunting. With each member of the family struggling to make a living and raise his own family, I don't know that it's going to be possible. Nobody knows for sure where it might lead, but most are betting it won't be good for deer hunting or deer hunters.

Portrait of a young man at deer camp.

We also visited the camp of my uncle Jim Genovesi and his friends, Wayne and Mike Johnston. I had hunted with them here in 1976 before they had the camp and they were sleeping in a tent. I took a buck that day and still held good memories of the place.

Jim's youngest daughter Kathleen is the same age as my daughter Erin and they have long been friends. That night as Jim cooked alligator and venison for dinner, the girls had a good time doing girl stuff while Nathan and Jim's teenage son Chris discussed deer rifles and hunting strategies like veterans. I had to leave, but my kids were invited to spend the night. It was an adventure for them to live, however briefly, without a tooth brush and to sleep in their clothes. In the morning Jim cooked them breakfast, served along with cake for dessert. Breaking the rules, if only a little, ensured that they all had a great time, which is what deer camp is all about. This is one of those camps where the kids feel welcome and wanted. It's a camp where deer hunting is secondary to good times. Most important, it is a camp where good memories are formed and families are strengthened.

Cleaning up after dinner, relaxing on the bunks before bed. Where else but deer camp can life be so laid back?

The camp is small and constructed so that it can be dissembled and moved at any time. Primary access to it is from a road that is now restricted by a gate. The landowner doesn't like hunters or internal combustion and forbids the use of their four-wheeler. This necessitates walking up the mountain in a long steep climb of almost 2 miles. There is limited access from the other end through the generosity of an abutting land owner who logged his land a few years back. To get the logs out he built a bridge across the brook, and roads nearly to the camp. But he restricts access to only Jim's and Mike's trucks and then to only a minimal number of trips in and out. In essence, they are all but locked out of using their camp because over the years land that they don't even hunt has been sold to people with a less favorable opinion of hunting and a more possessive attitude toward their land than what was traditionally held in Vermont.

domain. I can remember all too well the anguish of looking in on that club and being told I couldn't join right then. I vowed then that if I had children one day, they would never suffer the same pains. While I miss the rough "men only" atmosphere on a personal level, the new camps are better places.

But their future is uncertain in Vermont as the social changes that have invaded and mutated the very fabric of this state have taken a direction other than ours, the deer hunters'.

I question sadly if in another 30 years one of today's new hunters will be able to look back at deer camps and see the same strong memories and feel the enduring passion that I have been privileged to have lived.

If you'll forgive me for stealing a closing line from my favorite author: "Isn't it pretty to think so?"

While I mourn the passing of the deer camps of old and the demise of yet another thing that was for men only, I recognize and accept that these changes are necessary. If deer camps are to survive they must evolve. And if deer hunting itself is to survive, we must bring everybody into the fold. Society has changed too much for it to remain a masculine-dominated sport, or for deer camps to stay a man's

Southern Ridgetops & Riverbottoms

South Carolina

The Southern Deer Hunting Tradition

Deer hunting and deer camps are as much a part of Southern history as cotton and the Confederacy. Proud and independent, the people of the South have long held deer hunting a priority in life—from the Mississippi riverbottoms in Louisiana to the Blue Ridge Mountains of North Carolina and everywhere in between.

JIM CASADA talks about Southern deer hunting history and lore, tracking the deer camp as it has changed to suit changing Southern lands and lifestyles from pre-Columbus times right up to the modern day. Some of the focus is on Casada's native Carolinas, but overall this is a story of the entire South.

Come now on a historical tour, in words and pictures, of Southern deer hunting and deer camps, presented by a native son of the South.

The Southern Deer Hunting Tradition
By Jim Casada

THE BACKGROUND

Deer hunting's—and deer camps'—roots run deep in the Southern soil. From the earliest days of settlement, hardy pioneers hunted for sport and sustenance. Even before the first waves of European immigrants arrived, the whitetail loomed large in the culture of many of the region's American Indians. It was common practice among a number of tribes to employ what today would be described as "controlled burning" in order to keep lands open and green. These Southern prairies, as historians style them, were commonplace along rivers in the Carolinas and Georgia, and they are interesting because they remind us that rudimentary game management practices existed many centuries before the practice became commonplace among sport hunters.

A successful hunt, circa 1950s. American Indians hunted and managed Southern land centuries before this hunt ever took place.

The degree to which Indians depended on the whitetail over much of the region cannot be over emphasized. As one authority, Leonard Lee Rue, has noted, venison was their "bread of life." Intensely practical, the American Indians of the Southern woodlands and plains utilized deer to an extent that offers interesting ethical lessons to us today.

The hide was fashioned into clothing and was also used for shelter and a variety of accessories ranging from food storage bags to quivers. Sinew from the animal served as thread for sewing, and all sorts of tools were crafted from the bones. Hoofs and antlers provided glue, decorative items, totems, knife handles, weapons and the like. Even the hair was used for insulating carrying pouches for babies and to keep moccasins warm in the winter. In short, American Indians of the region utilized the plentiful whitetail to the fullest possible extent, and the entire lifestyle of many tribes involved a blend of subsistence agriculture and deer hunting.

Seen in that context, the tradition of the deer camp actually predates European settlement, for one of the most common approaches to hunting among Indians involved group efforts extended over periods of two or three weeks. To seek meat, the most skilled hunters of a tribe would venture far from the settled river bottoms where they raised crops. Even today, the practiced eye and knowing head can discern traditional Indian campsites along many rivers in the Low Country region of the Carolinas, and invariably archaeological "digs" at these sites unearth arrowheads and spear points along with pieces of whitetail bone.

Rudimentary game management practices existed many centuries before the practice became commonplace among sport hunters.

It is at once haunting and heartening to stand on one of these sites, usually an elevated spot at a river bend or where a feeder stream enters a major river, and listen to the distant hallelujah chorus of a pack of hounds hot on the trail of a deer. To do so is to realize that you are, at least from a hunter's perspective, treading on sacred ground. For it is true—though sadly few modern hunters are aware of the fact—that the favorite hunting grounds associated with deer hunting with dogs were once those of American Indians.

That means, in effect, that the Southern whitetail tradition reaches deep into the forgotten or little-known recesses of the past. As one takes a stand, deep down in a hardwood slough on a mist-shrouded morning in late September, it is worth pausing to ponder, full of wonder, about the ghosts of hunters who have gone before you at the same place but in another time.

With the coming of Europeans, thanks to record keeping and the written word, the Southern whitetail story takes on even more substance. Ample evidence exists to indicate just how prominently deer figured in life on the Southern frontier. Daniel Boone and Davey Crockett are but two well-known examples of what was a way of life in the South for the better part of two centuries. Individual hunters, such as Maryland's Meshach Browning, whose skills are immortalized in his autobiography, *Forty-Four Years in the Life of a Hunter*, may be less well-known but were no less skilled at hunting. Between 1796 and 1840, Browning killed between 1,800 and 2,000

Market hunting was common as Southern land was settled. Hunters shipped the meat to city markets or ate it themselves as they continued to hunt, gathering hides for sale.

deer, and the only thing truly extraordinary about this accomplishment is the fact that he recorded it.

Many other hunters had similar experiences but left no permanent record of the fact. Most were market hunters, supplying venison to city markets or, more commonly, using the meat for their own fare while selling the hides. In the latter regard, the records of the British Customs Service in Savannah, Georgia, for the period immediately prior to the outbreak of the American Revolution are instructive. Between 1755 and 1773 His Majesty's customs agents tallied shipments of deer skins amounting to 2,601,152 pounds (some 600,000 hides) from this one port.

In the state of Franklin, a forerunner to the state of Tennessee, official salaries were paid in deer skins for a few years, and across much of the South the hides were readily accepted as a medium of exchange.

Once again, much of this professional or market hunting was done in a fashion which, in its broadest sense, fits under the deer camp description. Commonly a few men—either close friends or from one or two families—hunted together for weeks on end. Carrying a few basics with them, and usually with the aid of horses, they would shift from one camp to another as they made dramatic inroads in whitetail populations. Preserving hides and drying or "jerking" meat was demanding work, but the rough-and-ready

lifestyle suited this special breed of man.

From today's perspective, it is well worth remembering that it was hardy souls such as these market hunters who formed the vanguard of America's westward expansion as we sought to fulfill our manifest destiny of peopling the continent from the Atlantic to the Pacific. The South and its deeply ingrained hunting heritage loomed large in the inexorable movement across the Appalachians and beyond. After all, hardened veterans of frontier hunting experiences turned the tide at Revolutionary War battles such as Kings Mountain with their sharpshooting, won a nation's gratitude with their exploits under the leadership of "Old Hickory" (Andrew Jackson) at the Battle of New Orleans, and garnered martyrdom at The Alamo.

Eventually, of course, relentless market hunting by highly skilled woodsmen took its toll, and the waning years of the 19th century were bleak ones indeed in the whitetail hunter's world.

The animal completely vanished over vast stretches of its one-time habitat, and the combination of a dearth of game and the advent of game conservation laws signaled an end to an extended saga of slaughter. The South was fortunate in that it escaped some of the worst effects of market hunting. Thanks to a comparatively sparse human population and vast expanses of land that remained a virtual wilderness, whitetails existed in decent numbers here even as they disappeared elsewhere. It was during this period, roughly stretching from the turn of the century to the late 1950s, that the lure and lore of the Southern deer hunting tradition as we know it today was born.

THE GOLDEN ERA OF SOUTHERN DEER CAMPS

Between the time when Southern deer numbers reached a low ebb around the turn of the 20th century and the advent of highly successful whitetail restoration efforts, old-fashioned hunting camps were in their heyday. This is something of a paradox, inasmuch as the relative scarcity of

Dogs and Southern deer hunting go hand in hand, and have for a long time. Proper planning of a hunt with dogs requires very precise, detailed maneuvers and strategies. These hunters obviously knew what they were doing.

whitetails might have led to the demise of a time-honored tradition. Yet that very scarcity resulted in vesting all aspects of the hunt with a special aura. Conditions demanded prolonged efforts and hard hunting for any real likelihood of success, and that was best accomplished by a number of men spending days or sometimes even weeks together in camp.

The precise nature of the camps varied markedly; the region, hunting methods and the hunters' backgrounds all played roles in shaping a camp's fabric. The last consideration was of particular note, so much so in fact, that it has been the basis of a serious work of scholarship, Stuart A. Marks's *Southern Hunting in Black and White: Nature, History, and Ritual in a Carolina Community* (1991). To understand the Southern deer-hunting tradition to the fullest, all of these factors must be kept firmly in mind.

"Huntermen" like this were highly skilled woodsmen who knew the deer, the dogs and the territory ... and how to make all three work together for a successful hunt.

There were two primary approaches or strategies involved in hunting deer. As anyone who has read one of the greatest deer tales ever written, William Faulkner's *Race at Morning* (one of four wonderful stories in his widely acclaimed book *Big Woods*) will realize, hunting with dogs is a deeply ingrained part of the Southern sporting culture.

A properly orchestrated hunt with dogs was (and remains) quite an undertaking. In some senses the planning that takes place prior to the actual hunt resembles preparations for a military campaign. Due attention must be given to critical factors such as wind direction and escape routes known to be favored by hard-pressed deer. Standers (those who are positioned in hopes of getting a shot at the driven deer) must be strategically placed as quietly and

A plantation house, typical of where the "Yankee sport" might stay on his hunt.

quickly as possible. Those handling the dogs—the real masters of the hunt (in days gone by, usually black men associated with or employed by the lead hunting family)—need to know their business and intimately understand the lay of the land. Even then, ultimate success is at the whim of a host of imponderables, such as the performance of the hounds, the alertness and marksmanship of the standers and the thoroughness with which the drive is conducted.

Hunts of this type were frequently associated with holidays. The glories of the Hampton Hunt—held at Christmas under the wise guidance of the squire of Hampton Plantation, Archibald Rutledge—provide a fine example.

Every year, as the Yuletide season arrived, Rutledge and his three sons, along with friends, neighbors and extended family, would gather at the Plantation, immortalized as *Home by the River* (1955) in one of Rutledge's many books, for the hunt. It was at least as much a social affair as it was sport, but make no doubt about it: A haunch of venison as the centerpiece to the family's Christmas

Day feast was of the utmost importance.

The night before the hunt, a sumptuous feast would welcome the participants. After the meal, plans for the following day would be formulated. These would involve not only the guests but the plantation workers often described by Old Flintlock (as Rutledge was known to his close associates) as his "black henchmen." These would be the individuals—the skilled "huntermen" like Old Galboa, faithful Gabe Myers, Phineas McConnor and the inimitable Prince Alston—who handled the hounds and followed them on horseback.

Woodsmen without peer, these men knew the quarry and its haunts intimately. Prince Alston, for example, was a man Rutledge described as "a companion to my heart" and "as close to nature as any man in the world," while Old Galboa often knew "what a buck will do before the deer himself does."

After much discussion and debate, spiced with a fair amount of friendly banter, plans for the next morning's hunt would be completed. Most holiday seasons, this drama would be reenacted sever-

... ultimate success is at the whim of a host of imponderables ...

there can be no denying his passion for the sport.

"With me deer hunting is kind of a religion," he once wrote, "and I have worshiped at this shrine ever since a grown oak was an acorn." He schooled his sons along similar lines, adopting a parental philosophy which held that "if a man brings up his sons to be hunters, they will never grow away from him. Rather the passing years will only bring them closer, with a thousand happy memories of the woods and fields."

There was another, quite different breed of hunter who shared the swamps, pine ridges and hardwood sloughs of the South Carolina Low Country Rutledge called home. These were affluent men from the North, universally known to the locals as "Yankee sports." In South Carolina especially, but also in coastal North Carolina and Georgia, these individuals acquired vast tracts of land, built lavish hunting quarters and hired full-time gamekeepers. Even today some of these clubs—high-brow harbingers of what has become a standard arrangement for many of the region's contemporary hunters—survive. In the yellowed pages of record books, lavish leather-bound prisoners housed in dust-coated glass cages, one can still read of and relive hunts dating back over the decades. They took place on lands owned by men such as Tom Yawkey of Boston Red Sox fame, members of the Rockefeller clan and Bernard Baruch, a close friend of and an adviser to President Franklin D. Roosevelt.

These "immigrant" hunters usually traveled by train, and their annual visits took on much of the air of a royal progress from the medieval era in Europe. No luxury money could buy was spared, and work for "the plantation" was a pillar of economic existence in many small, rural communities. There was some resentment of these outsiders, to be sure, and often the vast acres they owned were prime grounds for poachers. Yet these men, for all their wealth and for all the land they controlled, deserve no more than passing mention. In reality, they were almost an aberration, for theirs was an approach and an attitude well outside the mainstream of Southern deer hunting.

al times at Hampton Plantation, with similar hunts taking place at countless other locations across the South. For those interested in delving deeper into this sporting tapestry, one which exudes both the genteel hospitality and deep devotion to sport so characteristic of the region, Rutledge's writings capture it in his own inimitable fashion. In enduring books such as *Tom and I on the Old Plantation* (1918), *Plantation Game Trails* (1921), *An American Hunter* (1937), *Hunter's Choice* (1946) and *Those Were the Days* (1955), he captured the essence of the dog-hunting ethos to a depth and degree unmatched by any other scribe. The present writer has collected some 35 of his finest deer pieces in *Tales of Whitetails: Archibald Rutledge's Great Deer Hunting Stories* (1992).

Those who read Rutledge's work soon come to understand just how large hunts and hounds, mighty bucks and deep backwater sloughs loomed in his imagination. While his descriptions of deer hunts at times remind one of the old Southern adage which holds " 'Tis a poor piece of cloth which cannot use some embroidery,"

The Literature & Lore of Southern Deer Hunting

In a part of the country where storytelling has always been a cherished trait, it should come as no surprise that whitetail tales hold a sold place in the literature of Southern sport.

Without much question, pride of place in the regard belongs to South Carolina's Archibald Rutledge. Over the course of a writing career that encompassed portions of seven decades, Rutledge published hundreds of deer stories. Many of these are found in his books (he wrote well over 50 in the course of his lifetime), while others languish in forgotten obscurity in the pages of old sporting magazines. Two works compiled by his son Irvine [We Called Him Flintlock (1974) and Fireworks in the Peafield Corner (1986)] contain intriguing information on the joys of the Hampton Hunt, while my anthology, Tales of Whitetails: Archibald Rutledge's Great Deer Hunting Stories (1992), focuses exclusively on Flintlock and whitetails. [Editor's note: Inscribed copies of Tales of Whitetails can be ordered from Jim Casada for $24.95, plus $3 shipping and handling (c/o 1250 Yorkdale Drive, Rock Hill, SC 29730).]

Rutledge and Prince Alston in a grainy old photo taken just prior to a deer hunt. It is one of only three or four surviving photos of the great writer and his favorite hunting companion together.

Prince Alston, who was Rutledge's constant companion on deer hunts, was an individual Rutledge described as "a companion to my heart." Here he poses with an eight-point buck "Old Flintlock" (Rutledge) had just shot.

Long before Rutledge was born, William Elliott, in Carolina Sports by Land & Water (1846), provided an interesting look at deer hunting and other sporting matters. That portion of Stuart A. Marks's Southern Hunting in Black and White (1991) focusing on deer hunting (primarily Chapter 6) takes a scholarly look at the subject. While relatively small portions of Robert Ruark's The Old Man and the Boy (1957) and William Faulkner's Big Woods (1931) cover deer hunting, those that do are "must reads." Also worthy of note is Ruark's piece Dixie Deer Hunt, which originally appeared in the Saturday Evening Post and is included in a work edited by the present writer, Robert Ruark: The Lost Classics (1996). Another Tarheel writer on deer, in this instance little known, is Walton Stone. His memoirs, Walton Stone: A Bunyan, Boone, Crockett, A Robinson Crusoe (1931), contain all sorts of interesting and offbeat deer lore. For a more modern look at the deer camp and its place in the South, a work that promises to become a classic work is James Kilgo's Deep Enough for Ivorybills (1988). Also of interest, as well as being beautifully written, is The Deer Pasture (1985) by Rick Bass.

Details on all of these works, along with hundreds of others, will be found in the standard reference work Wegner's Bibliography on Deer and Deer Hunting (1992). This work is a gold mine of information by a serious student of the subject.

A more conventional Southern deer camp, containing the necessities for comfortable—if basic—living, right down to a spike-antler toilet paper holder.

That mainstream was the world to which Archibald Rutledge belonged, as did two other giants of Southern sporting letters, Robert Ruark and the aforementioned William Faulkner.

Like Rutledge, Ruark also gave us meaningful insight into the nature of the hunt during this "golden age." His book *The Old Man and the Boy* (1957) is considered by many the finest book ever written on the outdoors, while Faulkner's *Race at Morning* remains a classic statement of what the quest means to the hunter's soul. Interestingly though, the deer hunting they knew and loved was quite different from that experienced by Rutledge.

Faulkner's experiences focused on his annual retreat to a remote hunting camp, many miles from civilization, located in the Mississippi back-woods. Here he found welcome respite from the academic world of Oxford, Mississippi, or from the madness of Hollywood, both of which were outgrowths of his literary renown.

He reveled in the rounds of "bourbon and bull" around evening campfires in a rustic camp shack, and he had a deep admiration for the men with whom he hunted. They were individuals characterized by what he considered the hall-marks of the hunter: self-reliance, serenity of spir-it, unfailing courage and intimate familiarity with the wild world.

There is no better indication of how much Faulkner relished his days in hunt camp than his reaction when word of his having won the 1950 Nobel Prize for Literature leaked out in hunt camp (he had heard nothing about the recogni-tion; a late arrival brought with him a newspaper containing the information). The moment was formally celebrated with a meal of 'coon and collard greens, and during the post-meal period of conviviality an old timer posed a pointed question: "Bill," he asked, "now that you got all that money, I hear your head's so big you're not goin' huntin' with me anymore." Faulkner's response was a heartfelt one: "Hell," he said, "that's just money. They haven't got any deer meat over there" (in Sweden).

The rough and ready friendship Faulkner sought and found was unquestionably part of the magnetism of hunting and hunt camps. It was a time of male bonding, for youngsters to experi-ence sporting rites of passage, and for everyone concerned to forget, at least for a time, the cares and concerns of the everyday world.

Along with the actual act of hunting, the special foods and rituals associated with deer hunting were important parts of the overall experience. We have already noted, for example, how both Rutledge and Faulkner prized venison as a food. They also adhered closely to the time-honored rituals associ-ated with deer hunting—shirttail shearing for "low-shooting and no-shooting sports," as my grandfather once put it, blooding of a novice hunter in connection with his first kill, and careful division of the venison after a successful hunt.

But no one captures the feel and flair of rituals associated with deer hunting better than Robert Ruark. This staunch son of the North Carolina coast experienced the sport from a somewhat different perspective, for "deer camp" was a campsite rather than a building. Ruark's descriptions of the sort of meals cooked in camp are so vivid they literally start one's gastric juices to flowing.

And for those who have never been part of a deer hunt involving dogs, he captures the nature of the sport in delightful fashion: "Maybe you never heard a hound in the woods on a frosty fall morning, with the breeze light, the sun heating up the sky, and the 'aweful' expectancy that something big was going to happen to you. There aren't many things like it. When the baying gets closer and closer and still closer to you, you feel as if maybe you're going to explode if something doesn't happen quick. And when the direction changes and the dogs begin to fade, you feel so sick you want to throw up."

Ruark also describes the bittersweet moment of his first deer with power and poignancy. "All I knew then was that I was the richest boy in the world," he writes. "I cried a little bit inside about how lovely he was and how I felt about him." Later, as the men in the party gathered 'round for congratulations, he admits that "smug" was about the best word to assess his outlook.

"What a wonderful thing it was, when you are a kid, to have four huge, grown men—everything

A modern-day blooding ceremony, upon the taking of a first deer.

is bigger when you are a boy—come roaring up out of the woods to see you sitting by your first triumph." What followed their plaudits was the "blooding" ceremony, and again, Ruark's description says it all.

One of the adults "turned the buck over and cut open his belly. He tore out the paunch and ripped it open. It was full of green stuff and awful smelly gunk. All four men let out a whoop and grabbed me. Pete held the paunch and the other men stuck my head right in—blood, guts, green gunk, and all. It smelled worse than anything I ever smelled. I was bloody and full of partly digested deer fodder from my head to my belt." In the aftermath of the mirthful mess, the Old Man (his maternal grandfather), patted the youthful Ruark on the back and said: "That makes you a man."

The equipment and hunting methods may be different today (what would Ruark or Rutledge have thought of this rifle?) but a first deer is still a big milestone in a young Southern hunter's life.

For generations those simple five words have symbolized an important part of what deer hunting means to those of us living in the South. It affords a means for coming of age, for formal admission into the ranks of adulthood, and rituals ranging from blooding to the teaching of sporting ethics and safety. All form important parts of the process.

Of course, not all hunting in those days of yesteryear was done with dogs, although for some reason it is this aspect of Southern hunting that looms largest in the recorded lore of sport. The other face of hunting involved what was generally described as "still-hunting" or "stalking."

For most of the country, including areas of the South where dogs were not used or where dog hunting was not allowed, the solitary sport of still hunting had always held sway. With his emphasis on stealth and sound woodsmanship, the still hunter harkened back to the days of Boone and Crockett or, in a fictional guise, James Fenimore Cooper's protagonist in *The Deerslayer*, Natty Bumpo.

The "bible" of the still-hunting creed was Theodore Van Dyke's *The Still-Hunter*. First published in 1882 and frequently reprinted thereafter, it was, in the words of the leading modern authority, Dr. Rob Wegner, "an unsurpassed classic." He goes on to suggest that if "American deer hunters read this classic en masse, the future of the sport would be insured."

A lone still-hunter at his camp.

While many Southern hunters likely were unfamiliar with Van Dyke's work, they certainly practiced what his pages preached. For weeks prior to opening day, they carefully sought "sign," and in most areas deer were scarce enough for a rub or a regularly used trail to be a matter of some note.

Among those of this still-hunting persuasion, a curious blend of secrecy and sociability existed. Their "camp" really was no camp at all, but rather a gathering place from which hunters traditionally dispersed when going afield. Since much of the terrain where deer existed in huntable numbers lay within national forests, designated campgrounds with their boundaries often served as a meeting and greeting ground.

Here's an old-time deer camp typical of the still-hunters of the South's high country. By the looks of those trucks, it appears that this family brought enough provisions to stay awhile.

How well I recall, for example, the situation that existed in the high country of western North Carolina during my youth. On the Friday before the season opened on Saturday, as it always did, hunters from far and wide would flock to campgrounds in the so-called "hot spots" in the Pisgah and Nantahala National Forests. They would swap information (much of it intentionally misleading), tell lies, cook meals over open fires or on battered Coleman two-burner stoves, talk of conquests past and those yet to come, and maybe share a sip or two from someone's jug of "corn squeezin's."

Daybreak on Saturday would find the campsites deserted, with the last dregs of coffee cooling in the pot and hunters dispersed to all points of the compass. Virtually everyone got where he was going in the largely roadless and sometimes even trackless back country by "shank's mare" (a mountain expression for walking). Occasionally one would hear a distant shot bounce off the steep ridges and echo down the long hollows, but never was there the sort of fusillade that greets the dawn of the season's opener today.

The hardier souls or those with sufficient leisure—and their numbers were surprisingly large—would follow this basic pattern for one or even two weeks. Anyone who killed a buck, no matter what size, was assured of instant stature as a temporary hero, someone whose exploits would be the talk of crossroads stores and barber shops in his hometown for weeks to come. Those hunters who managed to bag a buck year after year—and they were as scarce as their quarry—became local legends.

Because deer were so few in number over much of the South, with vast swamplands in the Carolinas and along the Mississippi River being notable exceptions, there was an importance attached to a kill—any kill—comparable to the attention presently associated with record-book bucks. These were simpler days with much simpler hunting ways. The use of camouflage clothing was unknown, with most hunters wearing rough, noisy Duxback attire. Lures and masking scents were unknown, and hunters commonly took to the woods smelling of smoke, tobacco and maybe several days' accumulation of sweat.

Just getting one buck would have made the hunt a success, but these still-hunters got two. To accomplish the feat in the noisy canvas clothes-of-the-day they're wearing, their skills had to have been awesome.

There were no ATVs to get the hunter close to his destination, and in truth, anyone who deigned to use such transport (had it been available) would likely have risked being described as a "sissy" or worse. Treestands were unknown and scopes on rifles were a novelty. The weapon of choice for many hunters, thanks to the fact that it was the only gun they owned, was a shotgun. Loaded either with buckshot or a "punkin ball," the smoothbore was yet another of many limiting factors lessening the likelihood of hunter success.

Beginning in the 1950s and continuing apace over the next two decades, the traditions associated with both dog hunting and still hunting in the South underwent a determined assault. This was thanks first and foremost to restoration, which would in time result in one of the greatest wildlife conservation stories of modern times. However, major technological advances, dramatic changes to the rural landscape, and a remarkable shift in societal patterns were also part of the overall picture. These interacting factors mixed and melded to form a new

Southern approach to deer hunting, one which sees dog hunting in danger of relegation to the dustheap of history, and still-hunting, to a considerable degree, something that belongs to the world we have lost.

DIXIE DEER IN MODERN DAYS

With successful restoration efforts and ever-expanding whitetail numbers came vast changes to the Dixie hunting scene. Yet one constant remained—the importance of camaraderie, the caring, sharing and companionship—that has always been integral to the deer hunting experience in this region. James Kilgo puts this well in his first-rate book *Deep Enough for Ivorybills* (1988) when he states: "Whether or not I really want to kill the buck, I am not yet willing to forego the company of men who hunt."

Modern-day landowners, and holders of hunting leases, manage the land heavily. At left, this hunter is heading to a stand overlooking a food plot designed to help the area grow more and bigger deer (below). The traditions of dogs or still-hunting won't be involved in his hunt.

Sharing the joys and successes of a Southern deer hunt is as important today as it was a quarter, half or full century ago. The hunting tools and methods may be changing, but the goal—just to be there, in deer camp with people you care about—remains the same.

Bowhunting has made its way onto the Southern hunting scene, as it has across North America. The hunters of this camp lean toward tradition, though, with their recurves.

Kilgo speaks for legions of Dixie's deer men. So does Rick Bass in *The Deer Pasture* (1985), a book that takes its title from the name of his family's long-established Texas hunt camp. "On an opening-day Gillespie County whitetail-hunt," he writes, "tradition is as important as anything, perhaps even more important than the deer. . . . I firmly believe that my crowd—and they are a bunch of deer hunting sons-of-guns—would hold opening day deer camp in the J. C. Penney's parking lot if that's what it took to get us all together."

The "get together" mentality of which Bass and Kilgo write remains strong, but in today's South the setting is more likely to be a club than a camp. This evolution in the nature of the hunt comes directly from the tremendous upsurge in whitetail numbers. In the late 1950s and early 1960s, when this writer was growing up and when deer were few and far between, posted signs were almost nonexistent. As the deer herd grew though, posted signs proliferated like kudzu. In today's rural Southern landscape they sometimes seem to adorn every other tree and fence post, bearing mute testaments to the value attached to the right to hunt deer.

As timber companies and private landowners became increasingly aware of the economic benefits to be derived from leasing hunting rights, sportsmen found themselves on the horns of a dilemma.

For starters, the land available to hunters was decreasing on an ongoing basis, thanks to urban sprawl and strapped state wildlife department budgets that could not deal with soaring lease prices (today prime deer land in the Carolinas and Georgia, for example, draws lease fees of as much as $10 per acre per year). While it had once been easy to gain access to private land to hunt small game, deer were another story entirely. Indeed, hunters increasingly found themselves faced with two choices, neither of which was entirely palatable. They could either hunt on heavily pressured public land or join a club.

Hunting on public land almost certainly meant interference from other hunters on occasion; deer that became super spooky within days, hours or even minutes of the season's start; realistic safety concerns; and other negative factors, including a general lack of solitude. These were the prices one paid to hunt inexpensively. For those who valued solitude, worried about safety or simply wanted a high-quality hunt, clubs increasingly formed an answer. This option also came at a price, this time in the form of a hard hit squarely in the checkbook, with annual club dues ranging anywhere from a few hundred to several thousand dollars.

Yet there can be no denying the fact that yesterday's hunt camp, usually a remote site associated with wilderness or else a location on public land, has become today's hunt club. Some clubs have living quarters, but more often the "club-

The price is higher, but when it comes to hunting clubs, the quality of both the experience and the game often can't be denied.

house" takes the form of a long-abandoned tenant home that serves as a central meeting place and a location for a map of the club where hunters sign in before the hunt.

The map is a must, for it gives each hunter, usually on a first-come, first-served basis, a hunting area that is exclusively his or hers for the day. Other standard features of the communal meeting spot are likely to be a scale for weighing deer, a meat pole for hanging and dressing them, and perhaps a wire cage or box in which to store jawbones, if the club is involved in a quality management program. There may be a picnic table or two, and almost certainly there will be a fire ring for warmth at night, as well as the telling of midday tales. More often than not hunters do not stay overnight, inasmuch as members normally live within easy driving distance of the club. However, campers are commonplace sights,

This sign-in map shows which hunters will be hunting where, assuring that nobody gets in somebody else's way.

A meatpole of bucks from a modern-day Southern hunting camp. The traditions have evolved, and continue to do so, but the goal of getting a white-tailed buck and some good venison remains the same.

offering the opportunity to spend a night or two on site when desired, as well as a refuge from bad weather, a place for cooking or simply an escape from the confines of urban life.

Closely paralleling the switch from camp to club has been the way deer are hunted today. Dog hunting, sadly, is in decline, a victim of smaller land parcels, more people and the undeniable fact that neither deer nor dogs are respecters of property lines.

Likewise, there simply is not enough elbow room for the stealthy slipping and stalking, which meant that yesteryear's "still-hunter" really wasn't still at all. Instead, all across the South hunters utilize either fixed stands or climbers. Most clubs allow members to erect permanent stands, and these range in nature from elaborate roofed structures capable of holding two or three hunters, to simple ladder-and-platform arrangements chained to a tree. Where no trees of a satisfactory size are present, it is always possible to use a self-standing tripod or "Texas" stands.

More prevalent, especially on clubs founded in the last decade or so, is heavy reliance on climbers. Astute hunters realize that deer soon become wary of stands used repeatedly over the

A climbing stand: adding mobility to the modern-day stand hunter's arsenal. You're not stuck in one spot for the entire season anymore; move with the deer activity!

course of the season, whereas the mobility provided by climbers enables one to take that factor, along with others—such as wind direction or a newly located scrape- or rub-line—into consideration.

Another dramatic change is the way hunters get to their stands. In yesteryear they may have ridden a horse or a mule for a portion of the distance or employed the animals to get meat out of remote locations, but usually walking and dragging was the norm.

Today's hunter has four-wheelers to get him to and from the stand, help in bringing out deer, and the like (although some clubs do forbid use of the vehicles for any purpose except transporting a deer back to the club headquarters). Add to that the assistance of optics, odor-blocking agents, all-weather gear and the like, and the inescapable conclusion is that the

Getting a buck out the old-fashioned way (above) and the new-fangled way (right).

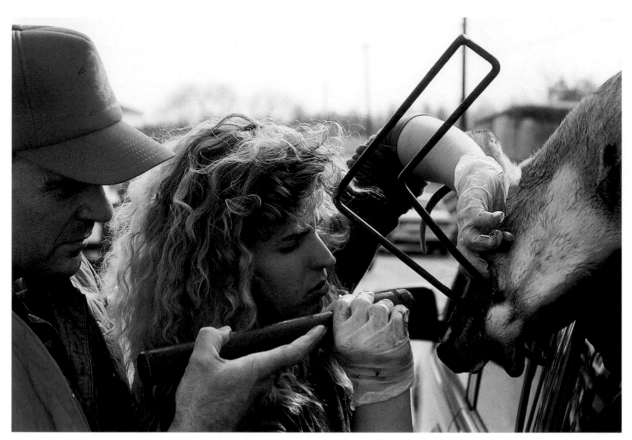

Herd management is more intensive today than it ever has been, both by the Southern states and by individual hunting clubs.

modern hunter down Dixie way is infinitely better prepared, in virtually every way, than was the case in the old days.

The "good old days" really weren't all that good when it came to deer hunting in this region. There were far too few deer, and today's hunter, in terms of likelihood of success, lives in a sporting Valhalla. The sheer number of whitetails goes far toward explaining yet another phenomenon associated with modern Southern clubs, that of quality management. It has become so easy to shoot a small buck, something which was once a feat of note, that many clubs have adopted rules designed to maintain herd balance and produce bigger bucks. The idea is to take plenty of mature does while being selective with bucks, letting them reach a reasonable age (at least 2½ years old) and optimum rack size. It takes time to grow bucks that will carry racks meeting the "quality" stipulation of a club.

These are but some of the many changes that serve as mileposts along the road to the way deer are hunted in the Southern heartland today; others which come to mind are growing participation of women of all ages, increased emphasis on primitive weapons and seasons devoted exclusively to bowhunting or muzzleloading, and the utilization of man drives (especially toward the end of the season when a herd still needs some thinning and some club members are anxious to stock their freezers with venison).

Still, certain constants remain, and these lie at the heart of the South's long love affair with the whitetail. The ritual of opening day, the special type of camaraderie offered by a gathering of hunters, the joyful rites of passage associated with a youngster killing his first deer, and the reliving of hunts ... all remain as changeless, as enduring in their charm, as the allure of the whitetail itself.

Western
Mountains & Breaks

Montana

Mule Deer Camp

Utter the words "deer camp" and—for many hunters if not most—whitetails, forests, swamps and fields come to mind. But follow Lewis and Clark's trail right up the Missouri River all the way to its source, and you'll find that there is another kind of great American deer camp—that of the mule deer hunter.

JOHN BARSNESS takes us to these camps, the camps of his lifetime. And in his straight-to-your-heart style, he makes them real, makes you feel like you were there too—up on the continental divide in Montana, floating down the Missouri, or hunting the badlands and breaks of a Colorado ranch a hundred miles from nowhere.

Barsness explores these mule deer camps and, maybe even more importantly, how his life, and many lives, would not be as complete without them.

Mule Deer Camp
By John Barsness

One of the great themes of literature has somebody young leaving home, discovering the cruel and beautiful world and beginning to ask exactly who they are—Huckleberry Finn starting his journey along the river of life. In the beginning, it is also deer camp.

Despite being born and raised in Montana in a town small enough that almost every year a moose or black bear showed up on Main Street, I grew up as something of a city kid. My parents were college professors and not terribly out-doorsy. Maybe once a year they'd pack up the tent and four kids and stay in a forest service campground a few miles from town. But the tent fit over the back of our station wagon, and later on was replaced by a trailer complete with propane stove and refrigerator.

Yellowstone Park was less than two hours away, but we always saw it through car windows or along the boardwalks above the geysers and hot springs, never far from the car. Our home movies of that time show a dozen different black bears sitting on a dozen different picnic tables, eating hot dogs or potato chips abandoned when we ran for the '57 Plymouth. At age eight I saw my first grizzlies through the windshield of that big old boat of a car—a sow and three cubs chomping down leftover pancakes behind Old Faithful Lodge.

So I grew up on the edge of the wilderness, yet somehow separated from it. But even through safety glass I could sense something out there, and

like my father the English teacher, I read all the time: an undisciplined mixture of Mark Twain and Edgar Rice Burroughs, Rudyard Kipling and *Outdoor Life*. Inside the Victorian brick walls of the Carnegie Public Library down the street were the make-believe of Tarzan's Africa and the reality of Jack London's Alaska.

All I know is that by 10 I owned a Daisy Red Ryder and was bicycling out of town to Hereford pastures where I could "hunt" the big-winged August grasshoppers, then use them to catch trout from Sourdough Creek. And on my 12th birthday, that edge-of-manhood milestone, I received a single-shot J.C. Higgins .22. That, however, was the year my folks were going to graduate school at the University of Minnesota, and we lived in the heart of the Twin Cities, where it would take two-day bike ride to reach someplace to shoot.

By the time we got back to Montana in June I was almost a crazed mountain man, even if my entire mountain existence lived mostly in my head. Looking back, I cannot imagine how my parents tolerated me. Maybe they didn't.

Make no mistake: Mule deer country is big ... and beautiful. Along the continental divide, Montana.

I was supposed to visit my uncle for a week that summer in tiny Virginia City, a near ghost town where he ran a summer theater. The week somehow turned into a month. For my parents it must have been a pretty nice vacation. I know it was for me, since I could walk out the door and into the ponderosa and sagebrush hills, .22 over my shoulder, rabbits and squirrels and the horizon my only companions.

But unlike Huck Finn, I had to return to school that fall, and could legally hunt deer that season. Now, my folks were not against hunting. My father had grown

By the time we got back to Montana in June I was almost a crazed mountain man, even if my entire mountain existence lived mostly in my head.

up on a Missouri Breaks homestead, and he lived on jackrabbits and sage grouse and mule deer as a kid. But he'd had a bad heart attack the year before and really couldn't help, except to occasionally drive me out to the Bridger Mountains and turn me loose for two or three hours. This, however, was usually where everybody else hunted on Saturdays.

But a solution presented itself. One of his students was an avid hunter, although a true urbanite, a refugee from New York City who'd come to Montana to search for exactly what I'd begun to vaguely perceive. With a small inheritance he'd bought a falling-down log cabin on a few acres in a canyon outside of town. He and his wife had rebuilt it into a one-bedroom home. He said I could come out and hunt with him if I wanted.

One Friday in early November my father drove me out there after school. By the time we entered the canyon, the cabin's windows were lit yellow in the gathering darkness, and pale pine-smoke rose from the chimney against a mountain covered by lodgepole pine and Douglas fir. My father stayed for supper (real venison, and potatoes from the garden), then left me with his .30-30 and drove back to town.

And I was left with Norm and his wife Sil, two adults a whole decade older. I helped wash the dishes and load chunks of lodgepole into the brass box next to the woodstove in the livingroom. Then, while Sil sat at the kitchen table and wrote out lesson plans for the one-room school where she taught, Norm and I sat next to that woodstove and talked about dawn. I got to fondle Norm's battered Savage 99, a .358 Winchester, and arranged my hunting clothes next to the couch, where I would sleep.

In the morning we got up in absolute darkness and ate eggs from their hen-house. Norm drank coffee. I had a glass of ivory-hued milk fresh from a Jersey cow belonging to a rancher down the road; yellowish cream that tasted faintly of cured alfalfa floated on top. In the dark we climbed the aspen coulee behind the house, toward the top of a long mountain ridge that ran all the way to the Yellowstone divide. It was a steep climb, and every 50 steps we'd stop and rest as the growing dawn showed the remnants of last week's snow under the pale aspens. And then we would climb again.

At the top we stopped and Norm lit a cigarette, then eased his rifle's lever down and quietly slid a round into the chamber, nodding at me to do the same. I nodded back, the first time I had partaken in the silent language of hunters. We waited in a saddle of the big ridge, the distant wheatfields of the valley below gaining a faint color as the sun rose closer to the Yellowstone divide. I could not take my eyes from that vista, stretching to the Bridger Mountains 30 miles away.

But soon Norm hissed. I looked at him and he pointed down the other side of the saddle, into the timber of the north slope. An old logging road covered with pine needles ran indistinctly up to our saddle, and in the middle of it were three mule deer. They stood there, black-gray in the still-dim light below the trees, big white rumps floating like ghosts above the trail, huge ears turning lightly like aspen leaves in a gentle breeze. Now I know they were a doe and her fawns, but then I simply knew they had no antlers, and so were not legal. Even so, my heart instantly loped through my chest like a cutting horse heading off a calf, working much harder than it had on the hike up the aspen draw.

We stood there watching. The deer walked into the big firs. No buck followed. We waited a while longer until we could really see into the shadows under the trees, then started down the trail. Norm motioned me in front. We heard ravens in the distance, and three times the tiny red squirrels of the Rockies scared the heck out of me, suddenly chattering above our heads. I had hunted them before with my single-shot .22, my first real game, my heart pounding almost as hard as at the sight of the doe and her children. But now I was a deer hunter, and found the lousy squirrels an annoyance, just like the writers I read in *Outdoor Life*.

Half a mile down the mountain I saw something move along the edge of the timber ahead of us, and half-raised my rifle before realizing it was a human. Or three humans—a man who lived up the canyon and his two teenage daughters, dressed in as much red as they could stand in those days before blaze orange.

We knew them—I went to school with one of the daughters—and walked up silently and whispered a conversation. They had hiked up from the other side of the ridge, their car parked down in an alfalfa field, and the girls were getting cold. The father wanted to hunt a little more, so while he headed up the mountain the girls headed down the road with us, toward a fork 150 yards below where they would turn left to the car, and we would turn right and hunt up another ridge.

The two blond girls were 30 yards ahead of me, moving fast to stay warm, when a buck mule deer walked out on the road just ahead of them. He turned and looked at the parade bearing down on him, and in panic thumped down the old road ahead of us. I raised my rifle while the girls ducked slightly, but I would have had to shoot 10 feet to their left, and never even cocked the .30-30. After all, I was a recent and highly-placed graduate of the Longfellow School Hunter Safety Class of 1966.

Behind me Norm quietly said a mild cuss word, then "nice buck." The deer looked enormous to me then, and for a few seasons after; now I know he was just an average 3x3 wearing his second set of antlers. But he would have been a fine buck to start with, and even now, when looking for venison, I search for him: a blocky 2-year-old with half again as much meat as a forkhorn, with the definite yet delicate flavor of a fat mule deer before the rut. After 30-odd years I can

see his big gray body whumping along that trail, two blonds in red between me and him.

We hunted the rest of the morning, but the weather was warm and the snow crunchy. Toward noon we headed back down the aspen draw, the unseen cabin far below us now, its woodsmoke hazing the dark timber on the far side of the valley.

While eating venison sandwiches at the kitchen table, Norm asked why I hadn't shot, and I told him. He looked at me a little sternly, obviously thinking the two girls were well out of the way, then finally nodded. That afternoon we went out again and saw no deer.

But when we sat around the livingroom after supper, Norm talked with me as if I were an adult, or at least more so than any adult ever had in my life. And that night in my sleeping bag on the couch, with the low fire burning black-and-orange behind the glass front of the woodstove, and all around me the level lines of the inside of a log cabin, I knew that somehow a part of me had left my parents' home.

Later that fall I spent another night in the cabin, then got up with Norm in the darkness and drove to a ranch where I killed a big mule

First deer, mule deer doe, long time ago. The smile still tells the story best.

Mule deer camp can take on the form of a ranch house, or even the ranch's bunkhouses. Although it's not in the aspens at timberline, a house like this, plopped here so far from anything else, is indeed a very special place to stay.

deer doe as she stood up in the timber 40 feet away. One lucky shot with the .30-30 broke her neck, and I was finally a real deer hunter. And after field-dressing her under Norm's supervision, maybe a little bit of a 13-year-old man.

I have lived in half a hundred mule deer camps since then, have slept under everything from the Milky Way, spread across the clear Rocky Mountain night almost as thickly as a glacier, to the high beams of a ranch house, chipped from mature pine by a broadaxe 100 years before. But only when surrounded by the horizontal lines of logs and the sifting of a pine fire do I drift back along the journey that began when I first left home for deer camp.

Unfortunately, log cabins are growing scarcer in Western deer camps, mostly because many of the places we used to build cabins are now filled with homes. Thirty or 40 years ago the folks that lived up the canyons outside of towns were either ranchers, who cut hay and grazed cattle along the creekbottoms, or the few town workers who owned a Willys Jeep or Dodge Power Wagon, with suspension as stiff as a John Deere tractor and heaters that defrosted the bottom half of the windshield but not the driver's feet. It took real pioneers to commute to town in those days, so most of the canyons held getaway cabins, not homes.

But just as air conditioning and Deet have transformed the Florida swamps into retirement villages, the modern 4-wheel-drive has transformed many Rocky Mountain canyons into a series of 5-acre ranchettes. It doesn't take near as much to live Out In The Country when your vehicle has push-button 4-wheel-drive, climate control, a CD player and a ride like a tailfin Cadillac's. Oh, and the main road's paved and a satellite dish—the "Montana State Flower"—sprouts from every yard.

So when a permanent structure becomes a deer camp these days, it's far more likely to be a ranch house or its bunkhouse. And it is far more likely to exist out on the high plains than in a Rocky Mountain canyon.

Glassing big country for mule deer bucks. The hunter stands next to some long-gone sheepherder's rockpile. Is it a landmark, or was piling rocks merely something to do?

These have also changed over the years. When just out of high school I spent one November working on a cattle ranch that also took in some "outastate" hunters during deer season. One of the deer-hunting headquarters was an old cow-camp line shack of maybe 8x12 feet. The prairie wind seeped through the tarpaper-covered walls, then sifted around the room in little drafts that touched your neck or ankle at odd and unexpected moments like an obsequious Labrador's tongue.

Along with the tongue-drafts, mice live there too. One older ranch-hand who doubled as a deer guide liked to startle the dudes by jumping up during supper, shouting "There's one of the dang varmints now!" and letting fly at an invading deer mouse with an old Colt revolver. He always got his mouse too.

Despite this the shack was free of .45-caliber ventilation, though if you looked closely you'd find the tiny holes of #12 shot around the mouse carcass.

The prairie wind seeped through the tarpaper-covered walls, then sifted around the room in little drafts ...

That was his secret, of course: tiny shot hand-loaded into .45 Long Colt cases. But many of the dudes never did figure it out, evidently having seen too many Westerns where the bad guys fall with no holes in their vests. Many headed home to New Jersey with tales of the old cowboy who shot the mouse running along the kitchen shelf.

But most ranch camps are more sophisticated these days, I'd guess since they charge more for the experience, though sometimes you'll have to share the bunkhouse with other stuff from the ranch's main occupation. By this I don't mean cowboys or actual cows. One fall four of us stayed most of a week at T. Wright and Polly Dickinson's

place out of Maybell, Colorado. Unlike the Colorado of Denver and Aspen, this is remote and uncrowded country, in the absolute northwest corner of the state above Dinosaur National Monument.

In the bunkhouse were stacked cases of canned beans and evaporated milk, because the nearest real town—Rock Springs, Wyoming—is over 50 miles away, much of it on gravel roads. And our Coors beer (what else in Colorado?) had to share the refrigerator with Angus antibiotics. But the weather was warm and there was a real shower, and each morning and evening we got to eat Polly's cooking and watch the Weather

Channel or maybe the University of Wyoming football team versus some unfortunate bunch of surfers and ghetto refugees from California.

Sharing a home with real ranchers is an educational experience for most hunters from other parts of the country. On various ranch hunts I have performed tasks ranging from unloading 40 piglets from a horse trailer to stacking hay bales on a flatbed semi-trailer. You may learn something about cows, but you'll probably learn more about the North American Free Trade Agreement, the black-footed ferrets just planted in the BLM pasture across the main road, and why Colorado ranchers hire Ecuadoran ranch hands. Turns out the black-footed ferrets are a blessing in disguise, because the U.S. Fish & Wildlife Service also sent somebody to shoot and trap the coyotes that eat the prairie dogs the ferrets live on—the same coyotes that tend to eat calves. But NAFTA is

First buck, ranch buck, out in the sage.

sending lots of cheap beef into the country, so many ranchers can't afford to pay local cowboys enough to work on a remote ranch. Instead they hire South American workers on two-year contracts.

You also learn the two sides of weather. Deer hunters hope for snow, which makes mule deer easier to find. But the Dickinsons were weaning their calves, and snow makes everything—driving, herding the cattle, working—a pain in the butt. But if you shut up and listen some, you also find out where the deer live, because ranchers who spend every week out in the hills know.

I found my buck in one of those places, a series of two-mile aspen draws splaying like fingers above the main creek. None of the other hunters in the area wanted to walk there. Almost all the land was public BLM ground, which you may legally travel with a pickup or ATV, and most of the other "hunters" seemed to do that—except down those rough aspen draws. So one morning after a light snow I walked down the longest draw and, by glassing ahead at every curve, found a big heavy-antlered buck bedded in the snow. A 100-yard crawl through the snow, a 250-yard shot with the .30-06 rested over a sagebrush, and he was mine.

But my hunting companion had bad luck. On the third day we found a big buck across a canyon, harassing some does. During the hour-long stalk he gave us the slip; the does were still there, but he'd wandered on. Then John missed a couple of smaller deer, which he normally doesn't do. By the time we figured out the scope had gone bad it was the last night, with only the next morning to hunt. I loaned him the '06, but who would loan him a deer?

At breakfast T. Wright said a big buck had been chasing some does by the stock pond near the ranch house. He'd seen him three days in a row, either morning or evening. Why not get up and sit on the hill and see what happened at sunrise? So John did.

About the time Polly started on the dishes we heard a dull thud from outside, down toward the stock pond, and 15 minutes later John opened the door and asked if anyone would help him load his buck. Now that is local knowledge. It turned out to be the same buck that had given us the slip earlier, a classic wide-antlered Colorado 4x4 three miles from where we'd seen him last.

But ranch hunting is nicest when you know the ranch yourself. One fall I was guiding on a place over in the ponderosa breaks of central Montana. My wife Eileen would come up every now and then and hunt the hayfields around the ranch house itself, and got to know the doe groups pretty well during bow season. She never did see a buck she wanted, though—just the little spikes and forkhorns that hadn't left their mamas yet.

> It turned out to be the same buck that had given us the slip earlier, a classic wide-antlered Colorado 4x4 three miles from where we'd seen him last.

This good buck visited a stock pond near the ranch one too many times and found a .30-06 rather than some does-in-heat waiting for him.

By the second week of November that always changes. I'd gotten that week's hunter his buck early and had a couple days off, so one evening after a 15-hour snowfall, Eileen and I started out from the house on foot. This was considered peculiar by the rancher/outfitter, a common attitude on the high plains, where a lot of younger hunters don't believe you can stalk a buck without a pickup truck. But we insisted, heading out two hours before dark.

Hayfields, the 10th of November and clear weather after a good snow are a fine mule deer combination. Even under the snow, the alfalfa is the last tender feed of the fall, which brings the does out to eat morning and evening. And the does bring the bucks.

We sat on the graceful overhanging curve of a sandstone rimrock, a small juniper at our backs, and started glassing. The hike had warmed us some, and in three layers of polypropylene and wool the four o'clock sun reflecting off the snowy slope below us felt pretty good. But when the sun went down the temperature fell fast, and my toes were starting to tingle when Eileen said, "Deer."

Even in the dim afterlight of sunset I could see them plainly at a half-mile, trotting out of the timber across the white expanse of a hayfield across the draw. And even with the unassisted eye you could tell one was a real buck, body twice the size of the does and antlers reaching above his head like leafless sagebrush. "Let's go," I said.

We dropped straight down into the draw and hiked fast in shin-deep snow, the dried seedheads of crested wheatgrass barely poking above the soft drifts. Silently we hiked hard to a line of big ponderosas next to the hayfield, easing up behind a tree just wider than our shoulders, Eileen leaned against it, then around it, raising the .270, and the does finally heard the slight scrape of wool against rough bark. Their ears turned toward us for a few seconds, high and rigid, and then the lead doe trotted toward the timber, and the others began to follow.

But the buck hesitated, perhaps wondering if we were an even friendlier doe. It was almost dark now, the deer near black against the white snow.

Eileen aimed and aimed and I, in my typical understanding way, whispered, "He's not going to stand there forever." She turned and gave me one quick glance that was not particularly friendly, then looked through the scope again and killed him. At the snow-dulled sound of the shot his hind legs collapsed, and then the front, his high-racked head tipping backwards as he fell. She ran another round into the chamber and we waited in the absolute stillness for a while until it was plain that this part of the hunt was over, then we walked over and looked at his big, thick-shouldered body. She counted the tines on his antlers, five on one side and six on the other, smiling at me, now understanding my urgency. We tagged and gutted him, washed our hands in the snow, and in starlight walked back down the draw to the house.

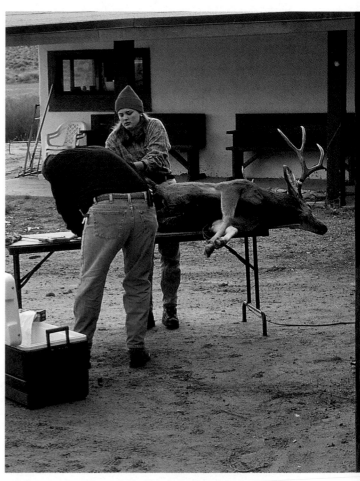

Skinning out a buck, back at the ranch. Ranch yards serve a wide variety of purposes over the course of a year. Today, this yard becomes a butcher shop.

I thought about that while falling asleep that night, as the buck hung cooling from the rafters of the ranch shop: how good it always feels to walk out from camp, find a deer and then walk back again. Of course the rancher had insisted on bringing in the buck by pickup, and while this was not the same as dragging him behind a horse, the rope from the saddle-horn stretched taut under your thigh, it was okay. And then I realized that the wall next to the bed was made of logs, and the soft sound I heard was not Eileen's tired breathing but the sifting of a pine fire, burning itself out in the fireplace of the big room outside our door. And then I was asleep too.

Even more satisfying is traveling by foot, or some other muscle, to a camp a day or two from the last internal combustion engine. The simplest method, of course, is to carry camp on your back, hiking until you find the right combination of level ground, firewood and water. I have done this, most often in the pleasant weather of bow season or an early October rifle season, sometimes just stretching a plastic tarp between trees and sleeping on the ground. If you've walked far enough, and aren't too much past 40, a bed of Idaho cedar needles does not make a bad bed, and a fresh blue grouse cooked over a fire does not make a bad meal.

Above: Packing in to the mountains, really getting away from it all, to camp and hunt. Right: Getting a blue grouse ready for a makeshift spit and a good fire. Real meat, much better than just freeze-dried macaroni and cheese.

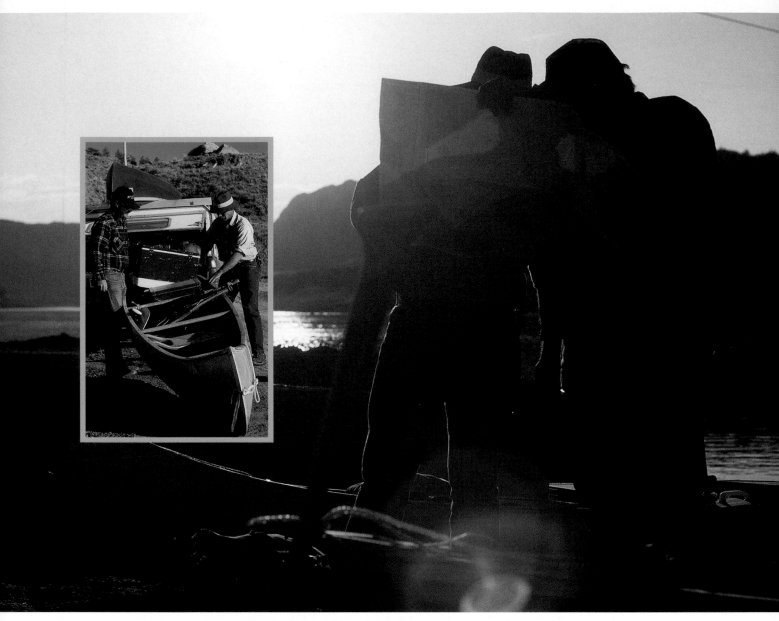

Inset: Unloading canoes and gear for a float down the Missouri. Above: Mapping out a plan. The first day's goal is to just to get around a few riverbends and leave any signs of civilization totally behind.

But somehow that is not real deer season. I grew up hoping for cold and snow, and still would rather kill a thick-necked buck in late October or November, when the nights turn frosty enough to chill the meat inside the deer's own hide, when you don't have to worry about flies on the steaks. So more often a friend and I push canoes into the current of a big river, canoes filled with far more amenities than a backpack, if somewhat fewer than a ranch house.

Our favorite place is a stretch of the Missouri River where Lewis and Clark traveled, and we take a copy of their Journals and a map from the BLM that marks the old campsites as nearly as they can be placed, nearly two centuries later. The first day is filled with long and complicated pickup shuttles, leaving one truck down where we'll come out, a week or so later. So the first afternoon's float is just far enough to get us around a few bends and away from any sign of what passes for civilization in what remains pretty wild country, though now empty of the grizzly bears and Blackfeet that Lewis and Clark encountered.

We do this often enough that, even if two or three years passes between trips, everything loads into the canoes easily, the places for the gas stove, the two coolers, the plywood kitchen box, sleeping bags and rifle cases all remembered from trips past. And after nosing the canoes into shore near some cottonwoods the sequence is the same: Milo setting up the dome tent while I keep hauling gear, then whoever is done first building a fire with driftwood from along the shore.

It's actually a pretty decent way to travel while hunting, since you paddle downstream during midday while the deer sleep, hunting the early mornings and late afternoons. But several days of it explains a few things about Lewis and Clark too. Before canoe-tramping the Missouri I never could figure out why so many of the Corps of Discovery went to bed without shelter, either from mosquitoes or weather. They did this because they were tired, because paddling a river through a head wind or snow squalls is damned hard work. And after putting into shore you've got to make camp, and always uphill from the river.

Above: The bluffs are steep, but you have to climb them to find the bucks. Below: Moving on to try another spot.

Mule deer camp, across the mighty Missouri. Below: Floating downstream to get where you're going isn't that hard, but loading and unlaoding, setting up camp and then climbing the steep bluffs to hunt is a lot of work, and hunters need some rest. Besides, part of the reason for coming is just being there, on the riverbank a long way from anywhere, alone with good friends.

So there comes a point where we stay two or three days in one spot, usually somewhere about mid-trip, as far from the places where pickup trucks can reach the river as we can get. You might think that because county roads pass a mile from the river in some places, along the bluffs 500 feet above, that we'd be relatively easy to find. But one year Milo's mother had a stroke and the local sheriff looked for four days and never found us. We didn't get the message until we ran into some other hunters, up on the bluffs.

So down on the river is a long ways back. Sometimes, with the little tent

pitched in thick willows to keep a blizzard from blowing it away in the night, or when the river starts to freeze and we have to break 10 feet of sheet ice to get the canoes into the channel, it seems too far. So why do we do it, especially since we hardly ever kill a mule deer?

I could be half-clever and repeat Sir Edmund Hillary: "Because it is there." But that would not be the whole answer. The whole answer would lie in big mule deer bucks, almost always not judged quite big enough to end our days

One nice thing about hunting the breaks is that if you shoot a deer, the drag to camp or the river will be downhill. A good plan would be to shoot him upstream too—you could paddle upstream a bit with an empty canoe and then ferry the load back down to camp. Once all that's done and the hunt is over, you can float out with your buck too.

Sunset on the river. Many explorers have gone this way, but the country is tough and the Missouri breaks in this part of Montana are still wild, truly a place that is Farther Back.

along the river. And picking up driftwood as we walk along the darkening bank to camp, after having just done our aerobic duty on another juniper-edged bluff. Or reading Lewis and Clark by lantern-light and falling asleep comforted by the dubious conceit of traveling by hand, just like them. Except, of course, for the gasoline lantern we read by, the canoes made of polymers, the nylon tent and scoped rifles. And you might, of course, point out that we almost never paddle upstream. That would be too much like work.

That search for Farther Back has made many Western deer camps more mobile these days. A great many ride behind the cabs of climate-controlled pickups. I have one of these myself, a minimalist pop-top, and it is quite handy, especially handy when the place you camped last year may now be somebody's subdivision. But traditionalists, those who go to deer camp for several days or even weeks rather than opening weekend, live in wall tents.

Tent camping seems to be losing favor in an America increasingly unwilling to give up central heating, refrigerators and Monday Night Football just because it's deer season. But those folks have never lived in a wall tent.

Notice the verb "live." In a good wall tent that is exactly what you can do. I have lived in the things for weeks at a time, far more comfortably than in any pickup camper I've ever seen, especially during cold weather.

Packing an entire camp—tents, stoves, food for hunters and horses alike and much more—into mule deer country. You don't just stay or get by in good wall tents like these horses are carrying; you can actually live there, comfortably, for a long time.

In a wall tent there's space under each cot for all your gear, a high ridgepole for drying wet clothes, a flat-topped woodstove that cooks fried eggs, sliced back-strap or (if you have any skill at all) the flat fried bread called bannock, far better than any propane cooktop. If your tent fits the number of inhabitants, there's room to get up from the dinner table without making everybody else stand too, or knocking over the syrup. And when you come down the mountain at night, snow

Above: Setting up camp. Below: A wall tent camp for mule deer. There's plenty of room for hunters, and even for the horses who brought you and everything else in and who will carry it all out.

One of the advantages of a wall tent camp: with room to stand and a full-sized wood stove (left), you can cook some real meals ... and then sit down to a table to enjoy them.

up to the tops of your pacs and air-bobbed soles slipping slightly at each step, there is a tent lit like an enormous orange cube and sparks lifting from the sheet-metal chimney into the blackening night.

Unless you're the first one back. But if you know what you're doing it only takes two minutes to light a lantern and build a fire, especially with a chunk of pitch-laden fatwood under the split lodgepole. Once that's done you have a few minutes to yourself, before the other hunters come in, to pour a little Tennessee whiskey into an enameled tin cup. By the time you take a few sips the tent is warming, some feeling is returning to your thighs after the steep and slippery descent, and you can start cooking. The others will be along soon enough to do their part, but because you were here first, making the tent orange and warm, somebody else will have to get up in the cold tomorrow morning to light the stove and lantern. And that makes you smile.

And then after eating, when the boots have been slid under the stove to dry, the rifles wiped down and hung by their slings from 16-penny nails driven into the side poles, you slide into a sleeping bag (or two, for a mummy bag inside a roomy summer bag is often best on a real late-season hunt) and listen to the popping of the fire and the wind in the trees and, well, the snoring.

In a wall tent there's no back room to segregate the big-time nasal symphony. Sometimes even ear-plugs don't pack it. The worst I have ever heard—so bad or good, depending on your perspective, that there is no close second place—is my friend Tom McIntyre. Tom is a big man and has an irrythmic snore that matches his body, resembling steam valves opening at whimsical intervals, quickly followed by the mating snort of a bull bison. But as they say on those TV commercials, wait, there's more!

When awake Tom is pretty talkative, and when he first falls asleep punctuates the steam and snorts with a few words, some as simple as "Huh?" but more often tending toward "Thatso?" or "Whatever." By about two or three a.m., he starts stringing words together into short phrases such as, "Life is its own self" or "Contrary to what Nietzsche claimed ..." Toward dawn he starts making acceptance speeches, or quoting long sections of obscure Czech novels. Some are amazingly entertaining, or would be if we'd gotten any sleep.

Once it got so bad that Jay Rightnour and I banished him to the back of his pickup after the first night. This helped—but not enough because the walls of his pickup topper were uninsulated, and his snorts walked through sheet aluminum and 12-ounce canvas like buffalo

As with any camp, snoring partners can be a problem. But the culprit is usually human, not canine.

through barbed wire. The next night we made him park the pickup 100 yards away. That finally did the trick.

So all is not peace and tranquility in every tent camp. One year Jay got some new custom-made aluminum poles for his 10x14, so we wouldn't have to pack half-a-dozen 16-foot lodgepoles on top of the pickup. Out in the badlands near the Dakota border, these went up far more easily than lodgepoles lashed together. We were congratulating ourselves when Jay noticed a minor flaw in the design: The wall poles were about six inches too long. The tent sat up above the ground like the calico skirts of a homesteader's wife.

No problem. We'd just get out the shovel and dig a six-inch hole under each pole. Trouble was, by the middle of November the ground tends to freeze. We got down a couple inches, then ran into a layer of frozen sandstone.

Well, we'd brought a bunch of firewood from the mountains where we lived, and with a roar going in the woodstove the tent stayed fairly cozy as long as we kept our boots on. But during the night things got interesting.

The deer mice hadn't gone to bed for the winter and found this large loose canvas canopy pretty interesting, especially since it was filled with cardboard boxes full of English muffins, Rice-a-Roni and cheap cheese. We took turns jumping up and piling boxes on top of the cold wood stove, often alerted by mice that ran up the wooden legs of our cots and across our heads. But in the morning we found that we hadn't heard them tearing the toilet paper to shreds. Whenever the wind came under the floor-gap during the next five days, creating a miniature cyclonic swirl, snow seemed to be falling up toward the ridge-pole. I kept finding dime-sized pieces of toilet paper in my hat and pockets, and once even in the magazine of my .30-06.

Bigger varmints can cause other problems. The ultimate Rocky Mountain tent camp involves horses and grizzly bears. One fall Jackson invited me along on opening week, up on the Rocky Mountain Front where few mule deer live, but the ones that do grow big. We packed in from an abandoned mining camp called Palookaville, past Two Gun Lake and then over the tundra pass and down through Slippery Hoof

Canyon into Badger Creek. In one of the few patches of sand along the glacial gravel we found a single grizzly print, maybe a week old. I asked Jackson if he ever had bear problems, since we were only 30-odd miles south of Glacier Park.

He shook his head. "Naw, these bears are all chicken-livered. The animal you really should to be afraid of is the one you're sitting on. Horses will kill you and never shed a tear."

Jackson, on top of the great divide, with a good mule deer buck.

On opening day we rode nine miles, and then dismounted and led the horses the final mile up Killemquick Gulch, up to the top of the ridge where the only things living in the fist-sized chunks of limestone are stunted subalpine fir and a few old anti-social mule deer bucks. We found one about 10 o'clock, feeding on the goat's-beard lichens hanging in the trees. After some slow following as he fed through the trees, I killed him as he walked over a low rise. We saw him fall, but it wasn't until I hiked over that I realized he was damn near as big as a spike elk, with perfectly matched 6x6 antlers that I still cannot imagine as being part of the luck of my life.

Despite Jackson's remark about the grizzlies, back at camp we hung my buck's quarters high on a lasso stretched between two aspens, 15 feet above the ground. The only part we kept on the ground was the antlers, which Jackson showed off to every hunter riding by. At night they lay at the foot of my cot.

About halfway through the hunt we started finding tracks of two small grizzlies down by the creek. And then one morning we found the track of a bigger bear right behind the tack tent. We started sleeping with our rifles at our sides, magazines loaded. But despite new tracks every morning, either down by the creek or around the tents, nothing happened, aside from having to ride further to catch the main horse herd each dawn.

Then we had to leave, and once again Jackson's contempt for the bears wasn't quite so strong. He was coming back in a few days to hunt elk, so we left the tents up, and packed all the non-perishable food into panniers and hung them from the aspen rope. We opened the tents up wide, to let the bears nose around if they wanted to. We buried two 50-pound bags of oats and rode the horses over the ground when we left. And then we rode out in a minor blizzard, the wind almost pushing us off the saddle as we crested the top of Slippery Hoof. By the time we reached the old cabin at Palookaville it was time to make some hot coffee laced with a little whiskey, and the meat from my buck was surface-frozen.

Jackson called two weeks later. "That big bear walked right through the back of both tents, ripping himself new doors. He made one in that back corner where your antlers lay. Then he dug up the oats and ate some and spread 'em around, and then he found a few beers we forgot in the creek, and pooped and puked all over the camp. There were piles of oats everywhere. I bet he had one nasty hangover!" Chicken-livered maybe, but smart. The old bear knew when the rifles had disappeared down the mountain.

Jackson was one of the best horsemen I've ever known, a man who in his youth not only made a big part of his living riding bucking horses, but knew how to break a wagon team and could pack up a two-tent camp in two hours, with only one or two adjustments needed over 15 miles of rough mountain trail.

And his words about bears and horses proved prophetic. Five years after our hunt he was starting his last summer pack trip of the season when his trusted saddle horse panicked at an unseen something and brushed Jackson off. He landed upside down, and that was that. And no, his faithful horse did not shed a tear.

Some would say he died too young, but hell, we all do. Life should be forever. That's what it feels like anyway, when you're up there on the top of mule deer country, above where even the bighorn sheep live, with either your hunting-hard legs or a good horse underneath you, and camp somewhere down a canyon near a creek, filled with whatever's needed for life away from telephones. Like me, Jackson was a semi-urban boy who could not stay out of the mountains. He grew up in Tennessee, a descendant of that other Jackson known as Stonewall, and had left home to find the wide world and himself a long, long time ago. He found both, up there in his mule deer camp on Badger Creek, which is a lot more than many of us can say. But if we begin the search at all, most of us end up in deer camp, sometimes here and sometimes over the Great Divide.

Southwestern
Brush & Deserts

Texas

Deer Camp, Texas Style

In a state with a deer-hunting tradition as rich and varied as Texas, where do you start? An entire book of this size might not be able to cover it all.

To get a flavor of some kind, photographer and writer **LANCE KRUEGER** *went into the South Texas brush. What follows is what he came back with: the stories of two very different camps—one a family getaway, the other a serious trophy-hunting operation with guides and a lodge and all the fixings.*

Maybe you'll get to Texas to hunt someday. If you don't, this picture-and-word tour will get you close.

Deer Camp, Texas Style
By Lance Krueger

Deer hunting in Texas is unlike any other region of the United States I have hunted. There is more diversity in Texas, whether in the variety of terrain, climate, hunting technique, management philosophies—or especially in the deer camps.

The reason is simple: Texas is huge and encompasses so many types of terrain. Texans will tell you that if you don't like one area of the state, we have everything you could want somewhere else. We have the oak-covered hill country in central Texas, the great forests of the Pineywoods in East Texas, the coastal prairies and marshes along the Gulf of Mexico, orange and palm trees growing in the semi-tropical jungle of the Rio Grande Valley, mountains out West, the badland deserts of the northern panhandle, and the thick scrub brush of mesquite trees and cactus in South Texas.

To give you an idea of how big Texas is, you could fit all of New England, New York, Pennsylvania, Ohio and Illinois within its borders at the same time. There aren't even blaze orange regulations in Texas during rifle season, since you seldom see another hunter after leaving camp on the expansive ranches.

In all these varied habitats live 4 million white-tailed deer. This is the largest deer herd of any state. More deer are killed in

Texas than any other state, and we harvest more deer annually than many states have in their entire herds. During one recent season, 371,332 deer were harvested by 613,279 hunters. That's a 54 percent success rate; and 59 percent of the harvest was bucks, the remainder does.

Known to scientists as Odocoileus virginianus texanus, Texas whitetails are uniquely designed for the hot climate. With smaller bodies, few fat reserves and short thin hair, they are built to displace heat quickly and stay cool in summer's brutal heat as well as the warm winters. Few Texas whitetails ever get to see snow in their lifetime. In fact, "cold weather" hunting here means temperatures in the 50s and occasionally some frost in the mornings. But even in December the temperature usually ranges from 60 to 80°F, and sometimes it nears 100.

If the Texas whitetail's antlers matched their body size, there would be little reason to hunt them, in many hunters' opinions. But the immensity of their bony crown is what makes the Texas whitetail so desirable. Most people traveling from other parts of the U.S. to hunt in Texas usually want to shoot the first buck they see because the rack is so large in comparison to his sleek body.

In fact, Texas is one of the leading states for qualifying entries into the Boone and Crockett record book, and is the only state to have had both World Record Typical and World Record Non-Typical whitetail bucks come from its soil. On a deer rack, an inch is an inch, and 170 inches of antler is the same size on a Canadian buck or on a Texas buck. Imagine a 170-inch rack from a 300-pound Canadian buck, then sticking it on a 130-pound Texas whitetail: You get the idea of why the racks look so big on Texas deer. It's because the racks are big! For example, a buck killed several years ago on the world-renowned King Ranch scored 239⅘ net non-typical Boone and Crockett Club inches. The 27-point buck dressed out at 105 pounds, and it seemed amazing that such a small animal could sport such a large crown.

Texas deer camps are as different as the habitats and fences that criss-cross the landscape. Accommodations could be anything from a hunter sleeping in the cab of his pickup truck, to the fanciest of five-star lodges with golden fixtures, crystal chandeliers and fine linens. On the fanciest of ranches, the lodge's amenities are endless, such as satellite television, gourmet meals, golf courses and indoor swimming pools. Heck, you can even be picked up right at the ranch airport by a Cadillac with a set of longhorns on the hood.

I will not show you the lowest or highest end of the spectrum here. Nor will I try to tell you that one is better than the other. In Texas, whatever you can afford will do. There are deer leases that are dirt cheap, and there are others that require you to be a millionare investing in the ranch. There are even some ranchers that won't let you hunt their ranch no matter how much money you are willing to spend.

After all, this is Texas and the pendulum is very wide-sweeping and large.

CASH FAMILY LEASE

The majority of deer hunting in Texas is done under a lease program. This is where you pay a rancher for certain hunting privileges for a cer-

> *Texas deer camps are as different as the habitats and fences that criss-cross the landscape.*

tain length of time, and for a certain price. You can either get a group of your buddies together to lease a ranch pasture or an entire ranch, or lease an open spot on an established lease and just fit in with the guys that are already there.

Despite the new popularity of "package hunting" in Texas, the majority of property is still under the tried-and-true lease system. According to Kirby Brown, Texas Parks and Wildlife Program Director for Private Lands and Habitat Enhancement, "Hunting is the ranchers' main income now, making more money than cattle. The lease system is what most ranchers use for hunting, and leases are keeping the habitat in place for the deer."

Deep in South Texas's Starr County, along the Rio Grande River, is a certain 1000-acre hunting lease, which is actually small by Texas standards. The land is owned by rancher Rene Vela and is leased by the relatives of the Cash, Risica, Morrow and Truax families. This hunting family has hunted together for the past 33 years on one lease or the other, and on the Vela ranch for the past 5 years. It is a year-round lease, and the game they hunt are deer, hogs, javalinas, dove, quail, rabbits and more.

The deer on this property aren't that big by

Deer hunting on the Cash Family Lease is a family affair, right down to swing sets for future hunters too little to take to the field.

Texas standards, but the traditions and camaraderie that prevail at this deer camp are extremely rich. I have been to deer camps all over the U.S. and Canada, and have never seen a more family-oriented deer lease than the Cash lease. The non-hunters and children are just as important at this deer camp as the hunters.

There are 10 hunters on the Cash family lease (two women and eight men), but they limit themselves to one buck apiece. Since they got the property after it was "shot out," they have limited themselves even further. The first year, Ron Risica didn't even see a single deer. A couple deer seasons later, they would usually only see 3 or 4 deer per day, but now they will daily see 15 to 20 deer per hunter.

The hunters are trying to build up the deer herd on the ranch, so they pass up does for now and some bucks. When there are enough deer on the ranch in the future, they will let young hunters in the family shoot does to keep their numbers in check. During one recent season, there were only four bucks shot: a spike, a 4-point and two 8-pointers. The 8-pointer was shot by Ron Risica and was the first buck he had pulled the trigger on since he started hunting this lease.

The Cash family hunts the way the majority of Texans hunt deer: in a box blind within eyeshot of a corn feeder. Other times they will spread corn down a *sendero* (Spanish for a long, skinny strip cut out of the brush) with a truck in hopes of drawing a buck out of the brush. Watching down fencelines near a feeder is another popular hunting technique.

By using a corn feeder, the hunters are actually trying to pull a hot doe to the feeder, and maybe a buck will escort her. Oftentimes the box blinds are set up at the intersection of two or more *senderos* or fencelines so that the hunter can see in several directions. In many parts of Texas, the brush is so thick that it is sometimes difficult to see 10 yards into it. This thick brush is the place deer like to live, particularly the mature bucks. So the *senderos* give a longer-range opportunity to see a deer crossing through an opening.

These are the senderos that cut through the South Texas brush. Without them, you'd have little chance of ever shooting a deer here. Below: Checking a corn feeder before the hunt.

Many people outside Texas may feel it is unsportsmanlike to hunt over a corn feeder, but think nothing of hunting at the edge of a corn-field in their own state. Before passing judgement on the use of feeders, remember that Texas is really a different place than the rest of the U.S.

Due to the warm temperatures, the thick vegetation grows nearly year-round, and is primarily what the deer eat. The deer are surrounded by this highly nutritious vegetation, which is also their "meat and potatoes." The "browse" (the tender ends of the brush) is their "meat," and the short weed shoots at their feet (called "forbes") are their "potatoes." The corn from a feeder is "dessert" to them, and may or may not draw deer, let alone a buck, out of the smorgasbord they live and hide in. In Texas you can hunt any way you want—stalking, calling or sitting—but most Texans prefer to hunt in a blind near a feeder. It is productive and allows for a clean shot from a known distance at a buck.

Camp life centers around a large porch attached to the barn-red cookhouse. It's warm enough here, even in deer season, that almost all meals can be eaten out on the porch.

In the rare case that a buck is shot at and wounded, everyone at the Cash camp comes out to track the deer and look for blood. The hunters will look night and day if need be. They once tracked a wounded deer for 3½ miles through three ranches (after getting each landowner's permission) before their search ended. If their dedication isn't rewarded with the recovered deer, then that hunter is finished hunting deer for the season.

The shirttail from his hunting shirt is cut off for missing but is given back to the hunter for a souvenir. If blood trailing recovers a young hunter's first buck, then his dad will wipe a stripe of blood from the buck on the new hunter's cheeks. Pictures will be taken of the hunter and his trophy, and he will wear his "stripes" proudly around camp for the weekend. These were the traditions and values this camp of hunters were raised with, and is how their kids are being taught.

The Cash families spend every weekend of the two-month Texas deer season at the ranch. And this doesn't mean just the men, or just the hunters; it means the whole family goes to the ranch.

Each family pulls in their own sleeping quarters. Most of these travel trailers will stay at camp for the duration of the two-month season, their owners arriving every Friday night for the two-day weekend hunt.

This deer camp is unique in the way it is set up, but similar to many deer camps I have seen because it involves people making the most of circumstances.

The camp activity centers around a building from the 1800s that is now the cook house. A family once lived here before the turn of the 20th century, and it is now considered a historical site. The color of the old building is "barn-red" with a large porch where several picnic tables are placed to keep family members out of the sun. All meals are served here, rain or shine. In this "camp house," Aunt Laree passes on a deer-camp tradition by showing her granddaughter, Allison, how to make jalapeño cornbread.

Every family has a travel trailer that sits in a row about 50 yards from the camp house. There are eight of these trailers. For the kids, there is a swing set, trees to climb, a small pond to look for animal tracks and plenty of cousins to play with. There are kids running around all over the deer camp area—catching insects and frogs, playing football and digging in the dirt to make a cave. There is not a single TV or video game in camp, yet you never hear the kids whining that they're bored.

The weekend routine is like this. All the families arrive Friday evening after work to eat together at deer camp. If a young friend of one of the teenagers is invited to deer camp for the weekend, Friday night is when the unsuspecting newcomer is taken on a snipe hunt, to "break them in."

Saturday morning the hunters rise early, hopefully without waking their families. The hunters gather at the camp house and decide who will sit at which of the ranch's 16 blinds. It is an understood rule that if you don't go out early to hunt, then you don't go out at all so you don't mess up anyone else's hunt. The hunters get into their blinds before daylight with only a cinnamon roll and coffee in their stomachs, hunt until 9 a.m. or so, and then return to camp.

By this time the whole camp is alive with kids playing chase and the wives talking over the latest news while comparing photo albums. If someone brings a buck into camp, then everyone helps out with the cleaning, skinning and quartering of the deer. This is usually done within an hour of when the buck was killed. The young kids usually fight over who gets to carry the bloody heart and liver from the cleaning station to the camp house. It is a camp tradition that the heart and liver of the deer is pan fried for breakfast, along with eggs, sausage, bacon, biscuits and gravy.

After breakfast, it's time for a midday siesta for the hunters, while the nieces hit up their aunts and uncles for Girl Scout cookie orders. By early afternoon, the hunters will be refreshed and will go out to spread corn down the *senderos* from Uncle Lyndon's pickup truck, for the afternoon hunt. Usually a bunch of the kids and non-hunting adults want to go for a ride, sight-see and help out. The kids are the ones to open ranch gates and are taught the responsibility of closing any gate they open. The older kids and adults get to keep their seats in the back of the pickup as they flick corn at unsuspecting riders. The kids learn that with age comes privileges, and that those privileges include watching young ones take care of ranch-gate duty.

In the early afternoon, camp members of all ages—hunters and non-hunters alike—go for a ride to spread corn down the senderos for the evening hunt. Gates are taken seriously here, and there are lots of them on the journey for young hunters to open and close.

By 3:00 p.m., it's time to hunt with the kids. The kids may shoot a hog or javelina, or maybe improve their marksmanship on rabbits. The non-hunters in camp will take other kids out to the blinds to watch birds and look at any wildlife that comes out of the brush.

This is also a time when adults teach their progeny gun safety when crossing fences, and woodsmanship while getting to the blinds. This woodsmanship often involves how to watch one's step for rattlesnakes.

Everyone will enjoy the abundant South Texas wildlife and a fiery sunset from the windows of their enclosed hideaway before heading back to camp.

I found out that Saturday night is when the real fun begins, and is why everyone is here at camp. While I was at the Cash lease, one of the brothers (who had already killed his buck)

showed up at the camp on this last weekend of deer season. He excitedly proclaimed, "I couldn't miss Saturday night at deer camp."

Even by Texas standards, the *pachanga* (Spanish for party) they put on can be rivaled at few other places. All the adults join in to get things together for the evening feed, while the kids play different games in various groups around the camp site. The men gather firewood and start a huge fire between stacked cinder blocks (which contain the heat and flames). While the men build the fire, the women gather and prepare the smorgasbord of food to be cooked. Each family brings from their trailer the meat and fixings that they brought for everyone to share. It resembles a potluck dinner at "Sunday church meeting." There is fried deer backstrap medallions smothered in gravy, fajitas, *tripas* (a Mexican delicacy, though I won't tell you what it is), hamburgers, grilled tuna steaks (from a previous family fishing trip),

Heading out for the evening hunt.

Left: Building up a cooking fire for Saturday night's deer camp feast. Below: All the cooking is done over the coals and flames contained between the cinder blocks.

cabbage, beans *a-la-charra*, corn on the cob, butter beans, pan-fried potatoes, pasta, green beans, chips and salsa. You name it, it's here.

And at the Cash deer camp, anything that is killed is eaten and this is stressed to the children. In the past, that has included quail, doves, rabbits, wild hog, javelina, and rattlesnake (tastes like chicken). Everything is cooked in large, cast-iron skillets and pots on a big mesh grill resting above the fire on the stacked cinder blocks. Beans are mixed, and fajitas are flipped. When everything is

Do they come for the food? The family togetherness? The friendship? The hunting? All these factors certainly play a role in making this one very special deer camp.

cooked, it's all put on a table along the outside camp house wall, and everyone fills their plates. A blessing is said over the food, and then everyone digs in. All eat until they are stuffed, and there's always food left over.

Then everyone hurriedly pitches in on cleanup duty, in anticipation of the fun yet to come. Dishes are washed while the teenage boys get to scrape and clean the pots and pans. They put the pots back on the grill covering the fire, and fill them with boiling water. Scraping and brushing the pots and pans is part of the "joy" of deer camp.

After all is cleaned up, the adults gather around the campfire to tell hunting stories. This is when some of the men break out a cigar and may have

Card games, storytelling, staring into a campfire, s'mores ... important post-supper activities on a Saturday night in deer camp.

Life's pace slows considerably here, part of the reason family members make sure to spend as many weekends as possible at deer camp.

a beer, the only time hunters are allowed to consume alcohol at camp.

Cousin Joey is a master at telling and mimicking the jokes of famous Cajun chef, Justin Wilson. Aunt Laree tells about the time she was on deer stand and couldn't "hold it" any longer, so she found the coffee can supplied in each blind for such emergencies. Squatting over the can, she was halfway through her potty break when a nice buck walked out. With her insulated pants and long johns around her ankles, she noisily got her gun up just as the buck headed for another part of the ranch. Everyone around the campfire laughed until they cried, though they had probably heard the story a few dozen times.

While this is going on into the late hours of night, the kids play a game of "Kick the Can" and then make "s'mores" around the campfire. Others drift back and forth from the tales around the fire to a game of Spades on a nearby picnic table. By midnight, everyone is in their family trailer, dreaming of the good food in their stomachs and the hunt in the morning.

Sunday morning brings the same morning ritual of the hunters getting up early to hunt one last time for the weekend, while the non-hunters sleep in. When the hunters arrive at 9, the breakfast feast is repeated. Then camp is closed down by noon for the week.

The responsibilities and fun times—as well as lessons learned—are the reasons the whole family looks forward to deer camp. On New Year's Eve, many kids around the world are blowing things up or drinking alcohol, but on that night the whole Cash family is together at deer camp. Deer camp, and the relationships they have with their parents, is why these kids aren't involved in drugs or drinking, and why they are just good kids—joys for me to be around, as they would be for anyone.

But this fun doesn't just happen during deer season. In the off-season, the families get together to build blinds and to put up feeders. They fish together, worship together and vacation together. The people in the Cash Family Lease are not just family; they are best friends as well.

TECOMATE RANCH

The Tecomate (Indian for "basket rack," pronounced "tech-oh-ma-tea") Ranch in South Texas has become rather popular in the past couple years after being featured in *Bill Jordan's Realtree Hunting* TV show and the *Monster Bucks IV* video. The focus of these hunting shows was on the tremendous bucks that live on the Tecomate.

But I want to show you another side of the Tecomate that is just as impressive: the people and the deer camp itself, which is located in some of the finest big-buck country in the world. I have been a guest at this whitetail honeyhole many times in the past while photographing and hunting by Gary's invitation. The Tecomate Ranch covers 4,000 acres on the county line of Jim Hogg and Starr counties, and manages another 7,000 acres of a bordering ranch.

Gary is a very successful oral surgeon in the cities of Harlingen and McAllen, which are about an hour-and-a-half drive from the ranch. Having hunted all his life where few deer were ever seen, Gary had a burning desire to own some "brush country" in South Texas, but specifically dreamed about owning a part of the legendary San Ramon Ranch. Gary felt it had everything

Far left: The main lodge at the Hooterville deer camp on the Tecomate ranch. The sign proclaiming Hooterville's existence (left) isn't fancy, but nobody really cares: The bucks here are fabulous.

an ideal ranch should have: close to where he lived, diversity of soils, good deer gene pool, thick brush, and land that could be farmed. The only drawback: The area had previously been hunted heavily.

Gary was still in his oral surgery residency in 1983 when 1,000 acres of the 14,000-acre San Ramon came up for sale. Since he didn't have his dentistry practice running, he couldn't afford to buy the property. So he got eight hunting buddies together and bought the first Tecomate South pasture (which became the name of the new ranch). Later the group would buy another 1,000 acres of the Tecomate North Pasture in 1986, and another 600 acres in 1988. In 1989 and 1990, Gary bought 1,400 more acres that he purchased himself. The same year the owners of the San Ramon asked Gary to take over the management of the deer hunting on the remainder of the San Ramon, which Gary leased to a group of hunters.

The Tecomate Ranch has two hunting lodges: the Tecomate ranch house and the Hooterville deer camp. The Tecomate ranch house was built when the partners purchased the Tecomate pasture. It is a rustic, Southwestern-style two-story camp house. It is the camp where investing partners in the Tecomate Ranch stay when they hunt.

But the camp we will look at is the Hooterville deer camp that has a number of houses, trailers and a lodge together in a deer camp community. The center of activity is the main hunting lodge, owned by Gary. The lodge is for Gary and his family when they are hunting and also for the "package hunters" (hunters that pay to deer hunt for three to five days) that are there to hunt on Gary's personal property of the Tecomate. The other trailer houses and buildings in the camp-limits of Hooterville are for the lease hunters. The Tecomate Ranch has about every kind of deer hunting access that Texas ranchers offer: leasing, package hunting, family hunting and investment partners.

When you're not out in the brush hunting, the lodge at Hooterville is more than comfortable. You can even watch a hunting video.

The Hooterville lodge's humble beginning was as a single-wide trailer house back in the '80s. It sufficed in keeping Gary's family out of the elements when they weren't hunting. But with Gary's constant view toward advancing the quality of his ranch, he began adding on. He added a living room with couches, easy chairs, a fireplace and a big screen TV with satellite hookup. Inside this Great Room are four bunkbeds, several closets, a dining table and an extra bathroom that is used by the package hunters.

After the addition was completed, they totally rebuilt the trailer-house part of the lodge and made it into a continuation of the addition they had just completed. They put in a kitchen and dining room, a guest bedroom and bath along with a master bedroom ... enough space to accommodate Gary and his family, along with up to four "package hunters" and four ranch guides. Package hunters that were in camp while I was

there said that they had everything they needed, plus satellite TV.

The man that outfits the ranch for Gary is renowned rifle builder Tim McWhorter from Georgia. Tim hires the guides and runs all the hunting operations for visiting hunters on the ranch. Tim also makes lunch after the morning hunt, and is it ever a delight. He usually makes his specialty: country-fried deer backstrap smothered in cream-gravy and spooned over halved drop-bisquits. This is a Southern specialty from Georgia. Let me tell you, it is absolutely delicious and is in itself worth a trip to the Tecomate.

For supper, a superb camp cook of Mexican ancestry prepares a meal for the hunters. Here you'll find some of the most delicious, authentic Mexican food you've ever tasted. Sometimes it's barbecued venison backstrap wrapped in bacon, or grilled fajitas (this ranching area of Texas is where the original fajitas came from), or *carne*

guisada y papas (Spanish for "meat and potatoes in gravy"), or big Texas T-bone steaks. With this goes all the fixings, such as tortillas, salsa, charro beans and Mexican rice. After dinner, we would sit up late at night talking about guns, about big bucks shot or missed in the past, and discussing hunting strategies for the next morning.

This deer camp is not elegant by any means. You won't find any gold fixtures or indoor swimming pools. But it is very comfortable and has all the amenities you would ever need, and it is one of the most functional deer camps for serious deer hunting you will ever find. And there are no phones in the lodge, so hunters can really and truly escape from their working world. Gary has chosen to invest the majority of his resources in the management of his deer instead of extravagances that serious deer hunters don't need to be comfortable and have a good hunt. Gary also employs one of the highest quality groups of guides and support staff anywhere.

When you come to the Tecomate, you are there to hunt big bucks and to give it all you've got. When you're not hunting, you're either sleeping, eating or watching TV. In the morning while the hunters are getting dressed, the guides have a "pow-wow" at the dinner table to decide the best places for the morning's hunt. Sometimes they even draw maps on a paper napkin or coffee filter, for some obscure stand. Hunters and guides are very serious about why they are here, and every effort is taken to get each hunter an opportunity at a big buck.

The guides are very serious here and work hard to get bucks for their hunters. Late at night, or hours before dawn, the kitchen table is the place where strategies are discussed and finalized ... and many successful hunts (often, hunts of a lifetime) begin.

Unless everyone is at the buck pole admiring a nice buck, Gary's lodge is the place everyone seems to gather after the morning or afternoon hunt. This is where you hear the camaraderie of the lease hunters that have hunted together for years talking about the day's sightings, as well as the "package hunters" telling about every buck they saw that day while with their guide. In a different group, the guides compare notes and talk over what was seen from different stands.

Nearly every buck the "package hunters" see is bigger than anything they have seen in their home state, and they usually see 15 big bucks in a day. Invariably, someone will hook up their video camera to the lodge's big screen TV to show off the bucks they passed up during the day's hunt. The major topic while watching this footage is whether a buck is old enough to shoot. This is the opposite of most camps, where the idea is to shoot first and take pictures later.

Earlier in the season, hunters from North Carolina, Florida, California, Arkansas and Georgia tested their skills against big bucks at the Tecomate. During my most recent stay at this camp, I saw serious trophy hunters from Mississippi, North Texas and New Jersey. There was also a father who had bought his son a deer hunt (donated by Gary) at the Texas Wildlife Association fundraiser.

Everyone in camp had a great time getting to know each other during their hunt, and even began to razz each other about being a "Yankee" or "Johnnie Reb" and jokingly trying to talk like each other. You would have thought these guys had known each other for years by the hard time they gave each other. And by the end of the hunt, each had become friends, exchanged business cards or addresses and hoped that they would share deer camp again somewhere down the road, maybe even again at Tecomate.

As far as hunting on the Tecomate, each package hunter has a ranch guide who knows the terrain and all the stands; this way the hunter has the most productive hunt possible for the few days he has at the ranch.

Hunters and guides eat together. The dinner conversation? Guess.

Until you've been to South Texas, it may be difficult to realize how "other-worldly" it is. The locals say that everything either bites, pokes or stings you, and that includes plant *and* animal life. Most out-of-state hunters are disheartened by the thickness of the 8- to 10-foot-high mesquite brush and cactus that you can see into only a few yards. Then they are overwhelmed by the distance of the shots they must make down the long, skinny *senderos* cut 800 yards through the impenetrable brush. Most shots on the Tecomate are 200 to 300 yards, with some in the 400- to 500-yard range.

But a package hunter's anxiety is somewhat allayed by the availability of an extremely accurate loaner rifle from Tim McWhorter that will shoot ½-inch groups. These 14-pound, "Tecomate Special" rifles were designed by Gary and built by Tim specifically for the long-range hunting on the Tecomate. Most of the hunters kill their Tecomate buck at a distance twice as far as their previous all-time longest shot on a deer, and is why most hunters don't leave the ranch without ordering one of these rifles.

In South Texas, the trees aren't big enough or straight enough to hang a regular treestand in, so the most common stand at the Tecomate is a tripod, which has a swivel seat and an excellent rifle rest and puts the hunter 12 to 15 feet off of the ground. These stands accommodate one hunter each, so two tripods (one for the guide and one for the hunter) are placed right next to each other against a mesquite tree to break up the hunters' outlines. This makes you a part of the woods instead of being screened off in a blind.

Hunter and guide in tripod stands on the Tecomate. Forget about trying to hang a treestand here! Note the rifle—a Tecomate special—designed and built for extreme accuracy on very long shots down the senderos.

> *In between the thin spokes of the long, skinny clearcut is the impenetrable brush where the deer live.*

It is a very exciting way to hunt, since it gives an elevated view, and the camouflaged hunter blends in with the habitat. Birds will perch in a tree only feet from you, while a bobcat may stalk a rabbit below your feet. But there are a few box blinds on the ranch for nasty weather, and even one blind that is 25 feet up the side of a windmill. Whatever the stand may be, the hunters carry with them strong binoculars (Gary uses the image-stabilized Zeiss 20X60s), spotting scopes (20 to 40X is recommended) and powerful rifle scopes on their long-range rifles. A bean-bag is placed between the gun and these elevated stands to dampen any vibrations, which are magnified with the strong optics.

These stands are usually set up at the hub of a wagon-wheel-shaped set of 4 to 8 *senderos* that surround the hunters. In between the thin spokes of the long, skinny clearcut is the impenetrable brush where the deer live. They only venture out into the *senderos* to walk across while traveling or chasing does.

Another favored way of hunting deer in South Texas is with the help of a "high-rack" vehicle. On the Tecomate, this is a 4-by-4 Suburban that has a fabric-covered frame that sits above the rig's cab. This custom truck is set up so you can even drive from this fancy crow's nest. These are rather popular movable blinds around Texas, and are perfectly legal for hunting deer.

Now I know you're probably thinking that we chase the deer down in these vehicles and then shoot the exhausted beast with our high-powered rifles. Well, that just doesn't happen. In the thick brush of Texas, the bucks just take two steps into the jungle of brush at the first sign of danger and disappear.

The high-rack at the Tecomate is used in three ways. The first way is to drive to a promising spot, park and watch. The elevated position allows you to see over the top of some of the low-slung brush, or down a *sendero*. The second way to use the high rack: drive it very slowly down ranch roads while scanning the distance for deer. If a deer is spotted, the driver stops the truck and the hunters evaluate the deer with powerful optics—if the buck stays exposed long enough. The high rack is also used to rattle antlers and call from the elevated position. The bucks that respond to the sound usually don't come in too close, but they will occasionally expose themselves enough so you can get a shot.

The high-rack serves as an elevated, portable blind of sorts. Without this vehicle, you could not see more than a few yards into the brush.

Rattling is also used in the tripods, in blinds and on the ground in the brush. When on the ground, the guide and hunter will set up in a cactus flat or along the edge of a *sendero* or natural opening where they can see a short distance. They will hide in the brush, and the guide will rattle while the hunter holds his rifle ready for the fleeting opportunity he may get.

Rattling was probably first used by American Indians when hunting deer, but it was in Texas that the technique became famous. The reason it works so well here isn't because the deer are programmed any differently than whitetails from any other part of the U.S., but because when a deer herd is managed properly, there is a proper age structure and an even buck-to-doe ratio. When such an age and sex structure exists, the competition for the available does is fierce. In most places around the U.S., there is a ratio of one buck to 6 to 10 does. When a buck has all the does he wants, there's no reason to fight for more than he can handle. I have successfully rattled in bucks in Illinois, Missouri and Michigan. This was in areas where the buck-to-doe ratio was even and there was a proper age structure. The northern bucks responded just as well as Texas bucks.

The biggest buck I have ever killed was on the Tecomate ranch. This high-racked 8-pointer scored 137⅞ gross Boone & Crockett points. The buck's antlers were very unique, with high-sweeping beams that gave the rack a heart-shape.

Lance Krueger and his Tecomate buck. Believe it or not, this is a "management" buck, culled from the herd because he had only 8 points at 5½ years of age.

Left: Occasionally guide and hunter will take to the ground for some rattling. The key here is to get as much of a view as possible, perhaps on a cactus flat. Still, you can't see far, and the opportunity for a shot can come and go in an instant.

This buck may seem like a really big buck, but is actually only average on the Tecomate. I saw quite a few bucks in the 150 B&C range, with several others in the 160s, and one buck just over 170, a true "Book" buck! And that was in three days of hunting.

The bucks I passed were either too young or had too many points! The reason I "settled" for the buck I killed was because Gary has rather strict guidelines for the bucks that are to be harvested on the ranch. The buck that I killed is actually considered a "management" buck, and is considered an "undesirable" in this deer herd. Why was this buck considered "undesirable," you might ask? Simply because the Tecomate has no shortage of big bucks.

Gary is not at the stage of trying to build the deer numbers, but is trying to "tweak" his buck herd. The buck I killed was "undesirable" because he was $5\frac{1}{2}$ years old (had reached maturity which is $4\frac{1}{2}$ years or older) and only had 8 points. But let me tell you, he sure made my heart beat!

With all this talk of managed deer herds, you may wonder how to get a deer herd to the point where it is properly managed. There have been entire books dedicated to this subject, so I will only touch on some of the basics used at the Tecomate.

For a buck to exhibit his full rack potential, three things have to happen. It's a sort of three-legged stool: Each of the legs is vital for balance, and without one leg, the whole thing crashes to the ground.

The first leg is "age." Tecomate bucks get to live $4\frac{1}{2}$ years before the managers even think about harvesting them. It's not until then that the buck has reached maturity and will grow his largest set of antlers ... if the other two legs of the stool are present.

The second leg is "genetics." If a buck's genetics are programmed for the buck to have 10 or more points, then he has a better chance of growing a high-scoring rack. But a majority of bucks have the genetics to only produce an 8-point rack. At the Tecomate, the hunters put a majority of the hunting pressure on these bucks with 8 or less points at $4\frac{1}{2}$ years or older—the "management" bucks. This way, the young bucks that have 10 or more points reach an older stage of maturity ($6\frac{1}{2}$ years old) before being harvested. These are the "trophy" bucks, with only a few of these harvested per year. In this plan, the older bucks with more points will be more dominant and make up a larger percentage of the herd, giving them a better chance of breed-

Rattling was probably first used by American Indians when hunting deer, but it was in Texas that the technique became famous.

ing. Plus, a "management" buck hunter, who may get to see one of these huge "trophy" bucks, is extremely excited to see such a rare deer. This is worth a lot to a hunter that will probably never see a buck this big in his home state. While I was in camp, some of the "management" hunters saw a "trophy" buck named Gordo (Spanish for fat boy) that was a "book" deer. They were nearly as excited about seeing this buck as they were about killing their own "management" buck!

The stool's third leg is "nutrition." In Texas, the magic word here is rainfall. The South Texas climate is extremely arid due to minimal rainfall, high temperatures and constant winds. (It was once known as the "Wild Horse Desert.") Gary helps out his deer herd's nutrition in several ways. During the good years when you get sufficient rainfall, and the bad years when drought dries everything up, the deer herd's rack-size rises and falls with the rainfall levels. Gary has devised a way to make the good years even better, and make the bad years not so bad.

He decided that for his bucks to be head and shoulders above other bucks on other ranches, nutrition would be key. At the Tecomate, there is about every type of food source a whitetail buck could desire: the incredibly diverse, nutritious brush that these deer call home; and high-protein, pelleted feed that the deer get from feeders evenly scattered throughout the ranch.

But pelleted feed, also known to Texas ranchers as "rain in a bag," is quite expensive to feed a large herd of deer on a year-round basis. So Gary decided that using dry-land farming techniques would be the way to supply this nutrition at a reasonable cost. He intensively researched and tested a variety of plants from around the world that would be able to not only survive, but thrive,

in this extremely arid region of South Texas during the hot summers. With the typically poor rainfall, this was an extremely difficult task to overcome without irrigation. But Gary finally found a plant from Australia that would thrive when nothing else would.

That plant has the funny name of Lab-Lab, and it thrives during the heat of summer, providing extremely high protein for the bucks' growing racks. With the high numbers of deer on this ranch, Gary had to devise a convertible, dual-height fence around the newly sprouting food-plots to keep the deer from eating the young plants to the roots. When the crop grows tall enough that the deer wouldn't decimate it, the bottom half of the mesh fence is raised to overlap the top half. Deer just walk right under the fence to get the nutritious crop.

During winter, Gary has a different set of foodplots made up of a mix of Austrian winter pea, Triticale, Hubam clover, various alfalfas, wheat, oats, medics and rye grass. These grow at different times of the winter and spring.

The combination of summer and winter food plots gives the deer a year-round food source, even in the worst of drought years. By selling the seeds of these plants to other ranchers, the Tecomate Seed Company is now at the forefront of the deer foodplot wave sweeping the United States hunting scene. [For information, call the Tecomate Ranch & Seed Company, Rt. 2 Box 77A, San Juan, TX 78589, (800) 332-4054.]

I have flown over the parched ranchland of South Texas during the winter, and the landscape can take on a desert-like appearance. But you can tell when you're over the Tecomate Ranch

Two good Tecomate bucks, two very happy hunters.

Tecomate bucks are huge in body by South Texas standards, with an average dressed weight of 180 pounds.

because of the bright green foodplots that nearly jump out at you, looking like the "greens" of a golf course. These green oases of highly nutritious plants attract deer when little else will. The deer don't have to travel far for this nutritious food since Gary has spread these plots across the ranch. These areas are no-hunting zones so that the deer aren't afraid to fill their bellies with the nutritious crops.

So what kind of bucks are dragged into the Tecomate deer camp after employing this three-legged management approach? In one typical year, ranch personnel harvested 55 does, and 7 "cull" bucks. The majority of the bucks that are killed are the "Management" bucks, and during the season there were 14 of these 8-point bucks. One 8-point buck scored 145 B&C. "Management" bucks' racks average over 130 B&C, with an average dressed weight of 180 pounds (55 pounds heavier than the dressed weights on most Texas ranches).

But the "cream of the crop" are the top-of-the-line monster bucks called "trophy" bucks that Gary and his family, the investors, the lease hunters and one or two "trophy" package hunters get to kill. Usually, only two package "trophy" hunters are allowed on the ranch, and that same year one hunter shot a 159 B&C buck and the other shot a 169 B&C buck—definite testimony to the success of Gary's foodplot program.

Trophy bucks on the Tecomate usually score between 150 and 180 gross Boone & Crockett points. For example, Gary's son Blair shot three bucks (164, 176, and 153 B&C), three years in a row that won first place in the youth division of the Muy Grande Deer Contest, a feat never

before or since surpassed. Each year since 1991, bucks from the Tecomate have won more than one category at Muy Grande. No ranch has ever done that. Plus, many bucks from the Tecomate have scored high enough to make it into the Texas Big Game Awards record book. Gary has brought the deer herd on the original 2,000 acres a long way. A helicopter deer census revealed that there were 6 immature bucks and 40 does on the property in the beginning—testimony that proper management of a deer herd works.

Texans love to brag about our state because there is a lot to brag about, especially when it comes to big whitetail bucks. Managing and hunting deer is our love and passion, and the deer camps are the places these philosophies are shared with other like-minded people— whether on the Cash Family Lease, the Tecomate Ranch or any other of the thousands of deer camps across the state. Traditions, fun, dedication and the need to "get away" draw Texans to deer camp, just like anywhere else. But it is the hunt for a big buck, and the enjoyment of nature, that draws us outside that camp's walls. This is testament to what deer camp is and represents to these people. To them, deer camp is much more than the confines of a building. It is the total experience of the hunt: having fun, getting out of town, enjoying nature, creating friendships, renewing relationships ... and waiting for a buck that will make your heart stop, out there in the quiet brushlands, deep in the heart of Texas.

Northern
Forests

Minnesota

Escape: One
Minnesota Deer Camp

As you travel northward out of the agricultural counties of Minnesota, Wisconsin and Michigan, you notice a gradual but definite change. The land goes from rich, soft and crop-filled to poor, hard and forested. The transition zone between the two extremes is maybe the harshest land of all—not really knowing whether it's farm or wilderness, with forest and wetlands usually winning the struggle.

This is the country where **RON BAHLS** takes us: to a deer camp in the midst of it all, there in a land struggling to define what it really is.

Put on your long johns and stoke the fire. You're going to east-central Minnesota in November.

Escape: One Minnesota Deer Camp
By Ron Bahls

It was 1965 and I was 12 years old. My father would hunt; I would carry a thermos of coffee. That first deer camp was at the end of a dead-end driveway, on a turn-of-the-century farmstead that had seen better days. Nestled under virgin Norway pines, the farmhouse served as headquarters.

I watched and listened in awe as Jake—the grizzled, white-haired, retired farmer—told story after story of putting the bead of his hexagonal-barreled lever action on countless bucks. Most of it was true, I'm sure, the racks nailed up everywhere on the place offering evidence.

A stroke had robbed Jake of the use of his legs. Sitting in a stuffed, leather-upholstered easy chair for hours, next to the old oil burner in the living room, I sensed a tinge of bitterness from him. He

This buck, circa 1950s, was shot by the author's father (right) in the farm/forest transition zone of the story.

The bucks aren't always huge here, and sometimes they're few and far between. So you take one when you can get one.

stared out the window for long periods, searching for something, maybe another whitetail ghosting through the tamarack? He tried harder to be a part of the group through his stories, knowing he wouldn't be out there dragging in a buck before anyone else, ever again.

His wife Olive possessed the kindness of an angel, and cared for us hunters like she did for her wheelchair-bound mate. Huge breakfasts in the large farm kitchen, remarkable dinners and generous bag lunches packed lovingly for each of us ... all because she wanted to.

Even more wonderful about Olive though, is that she hunted fervently right along with us. I've never known another woman so passionate about deer hunting as was this weathered, 60-year-old farmwife. Solid, strong and no-nonsense was her approach to everything in life.

Coming in late in the day, cold and weary, you could tell she was genuinely disappointed at not connecting with a deer, something she could provide for us and herself—as well as a way to prove her worth as a hunter.

"I sat down with my back to an old pine tree the good share of the forenoon," she slowly explained. "Thought I saw a little doe browsing in through the thicket, but she never came close enough for a shot," she said with her red-mittened hands caressing her old Winchester lever-action, also with a hexagonal barrel. She sure gained my respect that first morning! I made some drives while Dad missed an opportunity to shoot at a big-racked buck just as he dropped out of sight over a rise.

It was a full house, and rooms were in short supply. That night in the upstairs bedroom under old quilts, you could see stars through the wavy glass, and I listened to the wind outside and my dad's breathing next to me as he slept.

And I started to realize that there is no other feeling quite like being at deer camp.

By four, Olive was up again preparing oatmeal, toast, eggs, bacon, fruit, pie, milk and coffee to fortify us for another day in the woods. We gathered 'round the oval oilcloth-covered table and made plans for the coming hunt while flakes started to whiten the cedar shingles of the old dairy barn. No finer deer camp in all of northern Minnesota I thought, stepping out into the crisp November air.

When I finally did hunt with a firearm instead of a thermos in hand, deer camps evolved into some very interesting places. Take the old, wooden Agnes Hotel in Pine City, for instance. Built in the 1880s at the height of the lumber boom, the fine two-story building served many a woodcutter or traveler with a good night's rest, fine dining or spirits in the lounge.

But by the late 1960s there wasn't much glamour left in the place. The wooden floors creaked and cracked underfoot louder than anything you can imagine, and you couldn't find a flat surface in any of the halls if you tried. Old men with bushy white eyebrows hung out in the lobby, not speaking for hours on end: Just staring out the window, keeping tabs on the world going on outside their walls. A rope tied to the radiator served as a fire escape! There was little to no insulation, and all the rooms had transoms above the doors, so you could hear the neighbor across the hall as plain as if sitting next to him. I can't tell you some of the things I heard those nights at the Agnes, creaky old bedsprings notwithstanding.

But all in all, the old hotel did the job and got you through the night. Standing on a drainage ditch one morning at minus 10°F after a night at the Agnes, the bolt jammed when I tried to put another slug into my new shotgun. The doe looked at us for a long time, then walked off like we weren't even there. I could have used a hot cocoa in the Agnes' lobby about then.

The doe looked at us for a long time, then walked off like we weren't even there.

Numbing cold saved one doe in the early years: numb fingers and a jammed bolt allowed her to walk calmly off.

Then there were nights shared in the back of the '62 Chevy wagon out in the middle of wolf country. Not the best of nights before a hunt, they made the Agnes seem downright posh.

But Dad tried to make it comfortable for us, and I overlooked some discomfort for the opportunity to hunt whitetails. The next morning we noticed that the wolf tracks were as plentiful as the deer tracks! A bold little ermine investigated Dad's spot on a deadfall that day. It moved closer

and closer, until rattling him so, he never did get off a shot at the 10-point buck that was standing right behind him, a mere stone's throw away. On the same hunt, I lobbed a slug across a wide gully at a doe, never understanding the limited capabilities of the gun. She looked, looked again, then kept on walking like nothing had happened.

We kept coming back to that old station wagon though: to eat, sleep and warm up. It was our home base, our deer camp that year. For $11,

a "big game" license in those days allowed a hunter to take a deer of either sex, or a black bear. My secret hopes were to see a bear. In retrospect, I hate to think about three or four underpowered slugs of the day in an angry bruin. The gun would have been more aggravating than deadly, so it's a good thing a bear never showed.

We also spent some nights in the backseat of Dad's new '66 Plymouth Belvedere. Now there was a comfortable sleep: vinyl-covered foam with a sleeping bag over it!

Another below-zero morning with 4 inches of fresh snow on everything. It was a little tough getting started, waiting for the heater to start throwing heat while you sucked down lukewarm coffee from the thermos. It was a good hunt though, behind our old farm near Askov.

I started in the thick cedars down near the Kettle River, where the low branches and the thick moss carpeted the forest floor and made it dark and quiet with the new snow. A huge snowshoe hare called it home, and for a moment we stared eye to eye in the muffled darkness.

I discovered an abandoned deer shack someone had built years before. All the windows were gone, with a scrap of fabric blowing in the breeze, and the weathered gray wood barely hung on with rusted nails. Just room enough for two bunks. In my mind I could plainly see the old hunters hunkered there in their red plaid jackets, grinning and talking, while two bucks swirled on the meatpole outside. Long before blaze orange was ever heard of, these hunters of my dreams sported the kind of red that looks more like brown from a distance in fading light. Friends and farmers most likely, old timers with names like Johanssen, Wahlquist, Hassenfeld and Jensen come to mind; surely men of the land—second or third generation immigrants from Denmark, Norway, Sweden or Germany.

Their stories always circulated in town, spreading the news of the 14-point buck Kenny got, or the 295-pounder that came from Krogh's woods. Or the three-in-one-day triple that Uncle Oscar shot. This is the stuff that draws you back to the birches, pines and swamps year after year.

Holding on to the dreams, the stories, the heritage and the history makes you part of the rugged land—another Minnesotan on the roll of successful deer hunters, forever part of the landscape.

The abandoned farms were my favorite places to hunt: always plenty of treasure, like the old deer shack, left behind to explore or examine. There was usually plenty of deer sign to go with it.

I ended up looking out over a meadow from a hayloft, sitting on a pile of old hay. This was one of my better deer stands. No deer showed that day, but I soaked up the soul of that old barn for an afternoon, watching that lonely backwoods field, and came away a different person because of it.

The region I am talking about—this sandy-soiled, lonesome, brushy country where central Minnesota gives way to the North—is steeped in other stories too.

There's the one about how Jack Brown wore his fur coat in the woods, wanting to be warm against the wind. Someone shot him out of his tree stand, mistaking him for a bear. We still wonder: Did Jack wear that coat because he knew what would happen?

There was a desperate farmer, tired of the harsh life on the unforgiving land, who shot his entire family in the basement of the farmhouse and then took his own life, the only cure for his depression. Many fires destroyed barns and houses while the owners were away.

Brutal winters and tough times just "getting by" made some of these people tough and made others up and leave. The rugged terrain, covered with timber and swamps, had to be cleared. The abundance of glacial rock in the sad fields played hell with farm equipment. Bad weather ruined just enough crop to spoil your entire growing season, short as it may be. The life was not easy for anyone.

But through it all, the deer survived and prospered and the huge bucks just kept reproducing, growing bigger and bigger racks, and feeding more families year after year. "Go up there, if you want a big buck ... just ask ol' man Christensen if you can hunt behind his place." Or, down there on the Kettle, "someone saw a big 10-pointer there just last week." That's the way it used to be; a far simpler approach and much more fun to listen to.

Myself, I tried hard to find the deepest, thickest and most remote woods to hunt: places where you could walk for six hours and still not be certain where you were. There were, still are, plenty of places like this in this region: state land, uncharted tracts, areas as wild as you can imagine. The names of the towns read like this: Bruno, Kerrick, Danbury, Beroun, Askov and Kingsdale.

There were hunts where, if not for a good compass and sound mind, others may have failed: getting caught in a wet snow with improper gear or getting stuck in a rutted trail miles from any humanity, without a winch. These little surprises in life add something to the total experience. You learn to deal with it on your own, out there. If you've been there, you know the feeling.

I grew up, matured, became a better hunter and felt committed to the sport I had spent so many years developing. I learned which firearms were effective, which gear kept me warmest, and what tactics filled my deer tag. I traded a pair of 14-inch tires for the Marlin .30-30 Win. I use to this day. It had been used once, ironically enough, to shoot a bear. Since then, it has connected with 20 or more

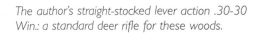
The author's straight-stocked lever action .30-30 Win.: a standard deer rifle for these woods.

deer. I doubt I could part with it now. It feels like an old friend after all these years.

There's just something about an old rifle. It's more fun to hold in your hands than a new one. But it can't be just old. Sitting rusting in a closet for years won't do that, won't add character. The rifle has to be carried to the woods, held in your lap for hundreds of hours. It should be shouldered, aimed, dropped, scratched, fired, misfired, cleaned and then fired again and again, all in the deer woods.

Later, I felt passionate enough about deer hunting to buy my own place, and hunt it. There was a lot of satisfaction and pride in knowing that this parcel of woods, no matter how small or imperfect it may be, would be my own preserve for all time. The whole experience of seeking, looking, making an offer, financing and ultimately enjoying your own place is like no other feeling. 1970s dollars went a little farther of course, but the $21 per month payment for my 10 acres seemed like a stretch at the time. The $11-a-year tax bill sweetened the pie just enough to make it tolerable, a risk well taken—one I would encourage any young naturalist to take if at all possible, because the rewards are immeasurable.

Minnesota's Snake River, nearing its juncture with the St. Croix.

As we clinched the deal, the real estate agent bought me a piece of cherry pie at The Grant House, an old brick hotel that was built in 1875. Looking back on it, he seemed a little nervous—partially because he was asking more per acre than the going rate at the time, I suspect, and partially because my age and appearance didn't add much to my credibility as a serious buyer. But things worked out. The loan was subsequently retired, and a cousin agreed to go in with me and purchase an adjoining 40 acres many years later.

According to the ancient abstract, the property was initially purchased by the railroad, and some great artifacts have been found after a little digging under the leaves. A vintage signal lantern seemed well preserved, minus the glass lenses. Pails, s-wrenches, bottles, you name it. Deep wheel ruts are still visible to this day from the logging trucks or wagons that came later; you can see them if you look "just so" along the forest floor, here and there.

The acreage also served as a cow pasture at one time for the closest hardscrabble dairy farm to our east. In fact, we still rely on the old four-strand barbwire as our lifeline to and from deer camp. It's the one constant in a flat, brushy but ever-changing landscape. Unearthed bones and an intact cowbell tell the story of one old bovine that didn't return to the barn one night with the rest of the girls. Antlered skulls and skeletons of whitetails appear occasionally as well.

Those first years we hunted the property were spent in travel trailers or tent campers pulled to the end of the road and propped up with rocks and bricks. Those '60s- and '70s-vintage boxes of aluminum, plastic, wood and

The last legs to deer camp. Driving this trail the final quarter-mile in, and then another hundred yards on yet a smaller trail, seals the thought: You're away from it all now.

canvas produced many wonderful times for family members and friends. Thank goodness for LP gas and 12-volt batteries. We hung our deer in the popple trees and celebrated with sodas and brewed beverages, like generations before us had. We donned our red and stepped out into the mist long before the nearest farmer was up for chores, the whir of grouse wings giving your heart a little start as you picked your way through thick brush on a rainy morning.

An over-the-cab truck camper was the next phase of shelter. The old LP heater was worn to the point where the cribbage board had to be called upon for duty: wedged in just right against the regulator, it kept the heat going steady all night. Even a mattress thrown in the back of a pickup bed, right on the steel and under the topper, worked one year. It never did fully warm up though. It's one of those life experiences that make you appreciate the finer things, even the simple things like a warm place to sleep.

But I longed for something better, something more permanent. You dream about the romance of a cabin in the woods, and one way or another, I was determined to see it through. Peeled logs were too hard to work with and maybe a bit too costly. What caught my eye though, was a barn kit of dimensional lumber that the franchise lumber yard offered. Wedged in the heart of farm country, near the confluence of the Snake and St. Croix Rivers, this acreage seemed like the perfect place to plop a barn design. I'd paint it gray, of course, the color of popple bark in the fall, so it would blend in nicely.

Deer camp, deer season, in the heart of the popple woods.

It would sit back off the road far enough so that no one would notice it. Through several months of weekend work, savings withdrawals and a talented brother-in-law, "the shack" was up and ready for the 1983 deer opener.

Since then we've modified it to our liking, so it fits our needs. We added a little insulation, a skylight, a sleeping loft (sleeps 2 to 3), a cupboard, a sinkboard and one of those '60s mother-of-pearl kitchen tables to bear our meals, elbows, plans and stories. An old easy chair sits in one corner, and if you shoot a buck you get to sit in it.

The racks of nearly all the bucks we've taken adorn the wall above the door as you walk in. The largest is a 10-pointer cousin Bob shot on a Sunday at 2 in the afternoon; the smallest, a 1-inch spike buck (probably a big fawn), mounted up on velvet as a gag, also taken by cousin Bob. Vintage tin signs, a bear trap, grouse tails, even a gray granite antique store bedpan decorate the walls and ceiling of this deer camp.

The boxwood heater has consumed hundreds of cords of dry birch, popple, oak, elm and ash cut right outside the door. The shack keeps the wind and rain out, lets us eat and sleep in peace; what else should this structure do for a bunch of anxious hunters?

Our numbers have varied from 1 to 6, which is about our maximum capacity. Our ages have ranged from 16 to 76.

The huge shipping crate of a printing press unit became the woodshed; with a door and shingles on the top, it's perfect. You can walk right in; I can thank a former employer for supplying this box-turned-woodshed.

We threw together a combination toolshed-outhouse with donated scrap lumber.

The work seems to never end, but it is all good work. We blazed trails and shooting lanes with chainsaws and bow saws. We constructed deerstands to our liking with scrap lumber or

Above: Just a few of the many buck racks above the door. Right: Grouse trophies—gathered on golden Indian Summer October days—adorn this camp's ceiling.

limbs cut on the spot. The annual graffiti added to these stands becomes more interesting as new bits are added and the old lines fade away. In them, we sit on pails or milk crates. We've worked together to repair and paint as needed. A peeled log became a flagpole, and split logs were laid up into a rail fence of sorts. An old handpump from a farm auction decorates the yard.

As much as the place itself and the sweat we've invested here and the people too have drawn us in, the wildlife keeps us coming back. The migrating woodcock were just thick one March while we were tent camping here. You could see 5 or 10 in any direction you turned. A mallard hen chose the foot of a nearby birch as a place to hatch her young one spring. We've watched a train of eight baby skunks follow their mother down a pathway, found a new-born fawn "hidden" just off the driveway, picked wild raspberries and strawberries in July and gathered wildflowers for dry bouquets in August, and we've shot grouse and woodcock here. We've seen bear, fox, coyote, hawks, owls, raccoon, porcupine and just about every other kind of bird or animal this area has to offer.

Spring work day: making firewood and, this year, building an outhouse.

In the spring we hold a work day and in the fall we hold a family day, where our spouses and children get to experience some of the allure and romance of life in deer camp. I think they actually enjoy this, but none would want to spend more than a night or two here. Visitors and relatives have come and gone from this place. Some have passed on, and it's nice to know they have touched our lives and this land in some way. Newcomers have been added to the group, as room allows: friends who share a common interest and similar style of hunting.

And sooner or later then, because time does not slow its march, deer season comes. We plan well in advance, setting aside opening weekend as a time to say "Time out, I'm going deer hunting!" Whatever vocation we busy ourselves with throughout the year, it becomes secondary for a few days in the fall.

It all starts when the shortened days and cooler nights send a message. The increased mailings from sporting goods companies gets us thinking about it. The newspaper articles and the cover photos at the magazine stand all send a similar message. Maybe getting out for a little small game hunting is the spark that sends the adrenaline coursing. Just the sight of a white-tail in September does this to me. Preseason scouting becomes necessary to the deer hunter. Being out there in the brush with thirty days yet between you and the opener is the kind of security you strive for. Seeing that first rub or scrape of the season starts to prepare you mentally for what is coming. In the end, it seems that the planning and preparation is about as enjoyable as the hunt itself, and others have shared a similar view with me.

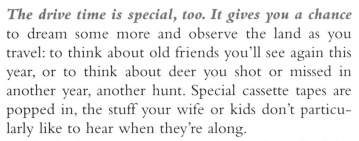

Finally, that Friday rolls around. Sleep was already lost on Wednesday and Thursday as you stayed up too late packing or running to the store for your share of the groceries. And to make matters worse, in Minnesota the weather usually turns for the worse just in time for opening weekend; it's just winter knocking. Will the snow make the trail impassable, or will the snow aid in tracking? Worries like that always enter in. It's exciting but nerve-wracking at the same time.

The last hours of work Friday morning are divided among concentrating on business and thinking of the hunt, as well as that something special about the trip itself. Going "up north" is part of the process, the phrase that keeps you going despite the feeling that you're going to explode with excitement.

Eve of the opener: airing things out.

I'm sure many of us could probably connect with a deer right in our backyards if we had to. But the excitement of the trip is part of the whole experience, and most of us prefer some distance between our home and where we hunt. I wonder, are there Canadian hunters that still have to drive "up north" to feel they are getting into prime deer country? In the end, "up north" is a way of saying "getting away." Most of us could hunt close to our own backyards, if we wanted to. But traveling from home to wilderness seems to be a required part of the process, one that makes deer camp and "the shack" special and different.

The drive time is special, too. It gives you a chance to dream some more and observe the land as you travel: to think about old friends you'll see again this year, or to think about deer you shot or missed in another year, another hunt. Special cassette tapes are popped in, the stuff your wife or kids don't particularly like to hear when they're along.

If a driving companion is with you, then all of this is vocalized, of course, and the tales get more exaggerated, the conversation louder, and thoughts shared that probably wouldn't get shared any other time of year.

Perhaps a meal at a café is held as well, in particular the Kaffé Stugga in Harris. The foods themselves—stuff you know you probably shouldn't eat—are promptly ordered up and savored. A little healthy competition with other hunting parties may ensue, flexing mind and muscle with others in a similar situation. As if to say, we're the Johnson boys from East Crossing, and we've been here, done that, shot deer and we know what we're doing. Every booth in the place has the same "Johnson boys." Just different names from different towns.

Nights of rest in deer camp seem to be something hunters secretly look forward to, and our group at "the shack" conforms. The rustic wooden loft with lumpy old mattresses thrown on suffice for some of us. Mouse droppings, dead flies or pesky moths find their way into the heart of the sleeping quarters, but it doesn't seem to bother anyone. A surplus army cot with a down bag on top makes a good deer camp bed, and now there is one of those newfangled, low-slung aluminum-framed cots too: the ones that always seem to rip out at the seams after a year or two of use. I hate to admit it, I actually used safety pins and rope lashing on my old army cot for a while, to eek out a couple more years of use. Bunched up

blankets or jackets for pillows get the job done.

All the old cast-off blankets and sheets from Grandma's house or Aunt Hilda's place find their way up to deer camp as well, but the main heat source is more often than not provided by wood, simply because there is so much fuel at hand.

Everyone loves the sound, smell and feel of a wood fire in a stove, fireplace or open pit. The nights I've dozed off with the hiss, crack and pop of oak on a slow burn are some of the best in my lifetime.

The second most popular heat source would have to be a propane burner in any number of configurations we have tried. Some are better than others, but all have extra safety considerations to

Deer camp's preferred heat source: the wood stove. Its sound is as soothing as its warmth.

consider. We don't worry about asphyxiation much at Bahls' Camp though: The construction was amateur enough to allow lots of air movement through any number of seams in the shack.

In fact, the worst complaints at our camp regard the smoke and excess heat more than they do being cold.

Once a barley pop or two is consumed, the final snack is scarfed, all the bladders are empty, and maybe even a few teeth brushed, there is nothing finer than lying down for that first night in the shack since preseason scouting. All the cares of your daily existence are out of the way. The battery-powered radio plays softly, the oil lamps slowly die down, and there is nothing but room to dream hunter's dreams for the next six to seven hours. Some of the preseason excitement and adrenaline have robbed me of more than one night's sleep before a particularly important season opener. If the weather forecast and conditions are right, there is nothing that will allow a man to relax enough to find sleep right away. But eventually exhaustion takes over, and maybe an hour or two of rest is all you'll enjoy.

Without a permanent well, we haul in the water supply in plastic jugs or coolers. Our tea kettle is perpetually full of water on the boxwood heater, mostly for coffee and hot cocoa. But a good measure of moisture is also put back into the room this way, the added benefit of keeping airways and throats from drying up altogether.

Then of course, there is the snoring. Nothing can get your goat as bad as one of your comrades beating you to sleep and then keeping you up with his blasted snoring! Some pretty heavy objects have found their mark on more than one occasion in our shack. But all is forgiven and forgotten next day … most of the time.

Wake up calls, battery-powered alarms, old wind-up clocks, and a few openers missed altogether are all part of that key hour or two before you take to the woods. We slept right on through 'til about nine o'clock one year due to failed batteries: a sinking feeling, all right. Bad batteries are my biggest complaint, producing so weak a signal that you'd never hear it, save your own internal clock telling you: "Hey, nimrod, it's that time of day you usually get up to go to work." Only this time it is going to be way more

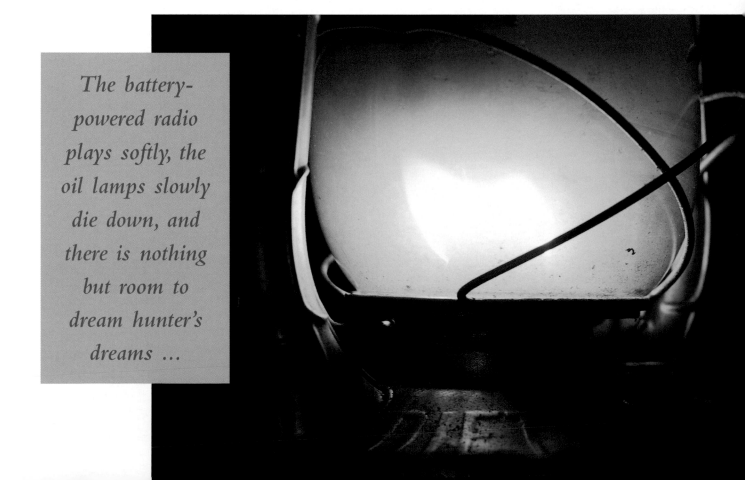

The battery-powered radio plays softly, the oil lamps slowly die down, and there is nothing but room to dream hunter's dreams …

fun, because you are going deer hunting!

The usual grunts, groans and stirrings in the sleeping bags takes place. Then clothes are wriggled into, the gear prepped and attempts at breakfast are started.

Actually there have been some very good meals served up at deer camp, and some very bad ones. We just can't seem to get breakfast done right with the Coleman stove. Old cast-off cookware could be a part of the problem. Hot spots and cold spots are always evident. Many a hunt has started with Vienna sausage out of a cold can. Always a little too hurried, as we are all preoccupied with the hunt at hand to do a good job on breakfast. Too bad, since this is probably the meal we need the most. One fellow thought quick foods, things you don't have to heat would be better. It worked, but it wasn't nearly as satisfying. So we try a new breakfast strategy every year.

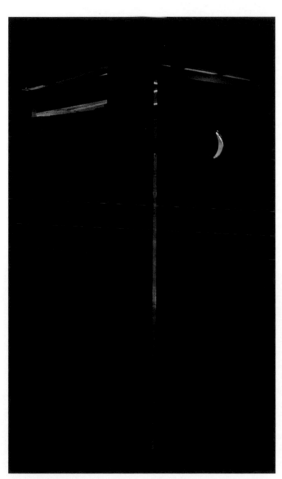

Everyone makes his trip to the outhouse, flashlight in hand. The ice-cold seat will certainly wake you up! The necessary paperwork resides in a covered coffee can so the mice can't get at it. One year a skunk or woodchuck filled in the hole with dirt, unbeknownst to us. By the end of the weekend, there was barely enough clearance to complete the job.

Then, one by one in the dark, we follow each other out the familiar trails and claim our stands, loading up our firearms and getting situated before the glow in the east ever begins to spread out over the aspen tops. Sometimes wild turkeys, making inroads into this rough

Above: Outhouse, an hour before dawn. Right: The dark and quiet trail out to the deer stands.

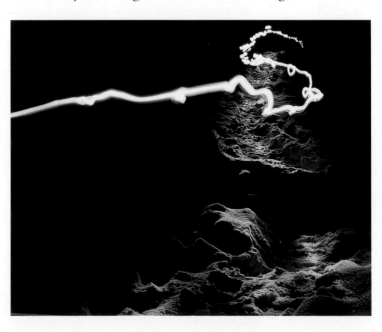

Many hours are spent in these stands and others—contemplating the things that hunters contemplate while waiting for a fleeting glimpse of brown in the gray brush as a buck picks his way through timber and marsh.

land, wait in their roost just long enough for you to get settled, then scare the hell out of you with their whipping wings upon departure.

Once you're in your stand, it's just you, your weapon, your brain and your thermos. Here is where the test is given. Can you sit still long enough to allow a deer close access? Can you stay calm enough to raise the rifle and put the crosshairs where they belong? Is the wind right? Can you remember to squeeze off the shot without jerking? Can you stave off the shakes with hot coffee or your own mind-over-matter?

One year a monster 12-point buck stopped directly underneath my stand in the darkness. With minutes to go until legal shooting light, I couldn't have lined up the sights even had I tried, for the blackness just wouldn't allow it. I can still hear his continued snort-wheezes fade away as the branches clacked against his headgear and he stomped off. Upon closer inspection later that morning, you could see the huge hoofprints planted next to the rock, sunk to the dewclaws in soft earth.

One year I had two good bucks, a 6- and 5-pointer, down within an hour of daylight. In Minnesota, if you're within earshot of a partner, you can "party hunt." This is the hunt I will remember when I'm old and gray. The rest of the party also fared well that day: a doe and a 4-point buck as well. We dragged our deer up to the meatpole behind the shack and worked up a sweat doing it, even though it was probably only 20°F outside. We cracked Pepsi's, smiled broadly for the camera and enjoyed camp life for a few moments that will matter forever. Five men, varied ages and sizes, vastly differing occupations and ideals, but at this moment we all felt the same joys. The sun was barely 45 degrees into

This is the hunt I will remember when I'm old and gray.

Bahls' camp members—and a few of their deer—through the years.

the southeast sky and the deer were cooling on the weathered wooden uprights—turning with the breeze as we counted our fortunes and felt ourselves rich.

Of course, we have counted our fortunes many times at this Pine County deer camp, and not just when the meatpole hangs heavy, for there are certainly years when it sags not one bit. So there truly is something special—even magical—about those twice- or thrice-a-decade days when *you* are the one whom luck has shined down upon, when *you* are the king of the forest skidding a buck down the logging road into camp after 3, 4 or 5 seasons of waiting deerless in the lonely woods. No, killing a deer

is not the only measure of a successful hunt, but if it didn't happen at least once in awhile, would we still come back? The pictures we cherish, of various bucks and does shot now and again down through the years, tell the story.

Some of us probably hunted some more that day. Others napped away the midday in the loft. As the sun started to set, our thoughts turned to the evening meal and the fellowship we'd share within the walls of that franchise barn kit. The Coleman would already be fired up, the oil lamps buring, and a great fire chugging in the belly of the stove. It's that kind of heat that radiates evenly, a searing heat that seems to find

its way into every nook and cranny in the place, and every sore, tired, cold inch of a human body benefits from it.

This is where a hunter can really relax. Take off the damp outer gear, put on a fresh pair of wool socks and have a hot drink. Ten or more hours out in the cold burning calories to stay warm generally take their toll on me. I crave warmth and food. Just ask the party I hunt with, they probably think I'm a real glutton, but everything tastes so good and goes down so easy after a hunt.

We have a great network of friends and wives who help out with the groceries and preparing main courses beforehand. Mostly, the hard work

is done at home on the Thursday before the season opens. So it is just a matter of putting a pot of antelope chili on the heater and talking until it bubbles and steams a little. Pre-packaged salads and foil wrapped bread complete an easy but satisfying meal. We all prefer to "rough it" just a little. Oh, on occasion we have all piled into Tom's Bronco and crossed the river into Wisconsin for a home-cooked meal in the local greasy spoon, but mostly we go just to gather deer stories from other parties, kid one another, shoot the breeze a lot, eat some pie, cake or other dessert, give the waitress a hard time, then head back to the woods.

After dinner and some semblance of a quick camp clean-up, the conversation continues. I can't even begin to share what topics we have all brought to deer camp. In your mind, put together whatever you want, because in reality, that's exactly what somebody is talking about in a farmhouse, travel trailer, motel room or what have you in deer country. We've even had a guitar and harmonica in camp over the years.

This goes on for hours, until finally somebody says it: "Well, I'm gonna hit it." With that, the party starts to lose steam fast. That 10-hours-in-the-cold thing—staring at the gray brush and fighting to stay warm and alert all day—is hitting everybody now. So usually before 10 p.m., sometimes even 8:30 or 9:00 after that first day of hunting, all the boys are back in their bunks: either snoring or thinking about the deer you shot this morning, or that flock of snow geese that honked overhead this afternoon.

I'm sure we even think about home or family. That's a normal thought—usually never work, though; it has been so far removed now through the events of the last days that it just isn't even important at that moment.

And what that means is: Mission accomplished. The whole event of the deer hunt has gotten you out of your daily routine.

The camaraderie shared in deer camp provides a bond that grows stronger each year. Every time you go through an experience with someone, you share and strengthen that common bond. A little melancholy may overcome you at these times, for the deer missed maybe, or for the one you thought was in the thicket but you couldn't quite get a look at. For the fact that the trip is half gone perhaps. For the partner that missed: If it had only been under my stand, what might have happened?

But before long the hiss of the teakettle and the crack of popple in the stove are once again the only sounds you hear. Sounds to dream by. I have thought often that I would like to record these sounds, much like the thundering rainstorms or field of crickets tapes you see at nature stores. Deer hunters would buy this stuff! I could put it on at home after a rough day and fall right off to sleep, no problem. Then there's that woodsmoke aroma that surely should be bottled in a cologne. Not the kind to wear on a night out with your wife, but to splash on before yardwork on a Saturday when you just can't get away from the confines of your home and yard. That woodsmoke richness, that fullness that you find comfort in, could be enjoyed without going all the way up to the shack ... or whatever deer hunting place you consider a second home.

The last days of the hunt are very much like the first day, but without that extra edge of adrenaline. Why? Because some of us have deer already, we've grown a little tired or impatient of the long hours with nothing to look at but the nuthatch pecking the lichens next to us. Personally, I've never felt a day hunting was a day wasted. Just enjoying nature and wildlife firsthand makes it worth the while for me. Experiencing the changing weather and light conditions is quite a show in itself. Throw in

The trail leading to deer camp—as to anywhere worthwhile—is not easy. Time is short, lives are busy. But making some time, and putting one foot in front of the other and just going, will get you there.

a downpour or blizzard for sheer excitement and you can say you've really lived! Make the most of it boys, for you, or it, could all be gone tomorrow.

They straggle in, for early lunches, to warm up, to put on dry boots or pass along deer sightings. The leftovers are cleaned up. The local AM station is broadcasting the Vikings or Packers game for our benefit. Sometimes, one of us will connect with a deer on Sunday or Monday or Tuesday. This animal never makes it to the meatpole. The last-day buck or doe bypasses this tradition, and gets lashed directly to the top of the Bronco or trunk lid of the Grand Prix, or thrown in the bed of a pickup. By 3 in the afternoon, we start to gather our things. Nobody really says it, but we all start to think about the obligations that Other World will bring. One guy pitches in to wash dishes in the round pan if there's enough hot water left in the kettle. Another grabs the broom and whisks out the leaves, sand, ash and crumbs that have rained

More often than not, all you go home with are memories of the quiet and lonely woods. And, when it comes right down to it, that's enough ... and it's probably what you were looking for anyway.

down on the plywood floor since Friday evening. The light starts to fade by 4:30, and soon the sleeping bags, gun cases, coolers and half-full 12-packs are loaded into the vehicles. In our state, the rifle season encompasses three weekends. Some hunters will get away to hunt again, others may not. "You coming back next weekend John? Yeah, I'll be here. What about you Bob? Nah, I gotta work."

After the high idles are kicked down, handshakes, thank-yous and goodbyes are finished, one by one the Fords, Chevys or Dodges wind down the lane back to the gravel, that leads to the blacktop that leads to the freeway, that leads to our various homes and varied lives.

I snap the old padlock back on the hasp. The wind sighs through the popple tops, spins the weathervane into a squeak and pulls a wisp of smoke from the galvanized stack as the last coals continue to die. Chickadees flit from branch to branch, and I zip my jacket against the deepening cold. Without even consciously

thinking about it, I usually have a word with the Maker for bringing us to this place, for the adventure shared, for the game taken and for safe passage back home. It becomes very satisfying at this point, as darkness sets in and the night sounds begin. I pull away, and deer camp becomes silent once again.

Eastern Woodlands

Pennylvania

Deer Camps of Pennsylvania

To someone from the Midwest, South or West, Pennsylvania might not seem like deer camp paradise, what with so many people and a good number of large cities and all. But if you live in Pennsylvania, or ever get a chance to really explore it, you know different: This place is beautiful, and there are a lot of deer here.

Of course, there are a lot of hunters as well, but that only makes the deer camp tradition even stronger. Pennsylvanian **TOM FEGELY** explores the state's deer camps for us and, equally as important, makes some insights into just what the attraction of deer camp really is—not just in Pennsylvania, but anywhere.

So throw your gear in and let's get going. Time to get to camp, Buck Season opens day after tomorrow.

Deer Camps of Pennsylvania
By Tom Fegely

Pennsylvania deer camps, like the hunters who inhabit them, come in a variety of sizes, shapes, smells, sounds and personalities.

Converted trailer or magnificent log cabin, remodeled farmhouse or comfortable RV, rundown one-roomer or pup tent at the edge of the woods, the camps all share one feature: They're palaces to the hunters who migrate to them every buck season.

A camp's value isn't measured by whether it's carpeted and water flows at the twist of a handle or whether the floor is grooved board and water is toted from the bubbling spring at the bottom of the hill.

Deer camp isn't restricted to cabins, snow and rifles. Family-style canvas tents, autumn colors and bows also work just fine.

In some places, billboards might not be seen by enough hunters to make a difference. Not in Pennsylvania. Plus, deer hunting is big business here. Safety is important so that you can hunt (and contribute to the economy) again next year too.

Perhaps the bathroom is walled in tile and the shower spits hot water. Or bath time—if there is bath time at all—may mean heating your own kettle on the woodstove, dumping the contents into a tin basin and washing one's "necessaries," as Pennsylvania Dutchmen refer to the task.

Of course, the lack of running water in deer camp strongly hints that there's nothing to flush. The nearest "relief room" is most likely a tumbledown outhouse—with an obligatory half moon carved through the squeaky door—some 25 cold and snowy paces from the cabin. Visits to the one-holers on cold December nights are understandably abbreviated. Magazines stacked on the floor are seldom read as one manages to get in and out in a minimum of time, guided by a flashlight's beam.

Outhouses continue to be deer camp standards whether they're needed or not, as if permitted to stand and function as a tribute to the past long after indoor plumbing's been installed. No deer camp is complete without the identifi-

able structure "out back," where it belongs.

Deer camps are what hunters make of them. In Pennsylvania, they make memories.

The exodus begins on Thanksgiving Day for those not obligated to be home for turkey dinner. More likely, the roast gobbler is quickly gobbled, you kiss your wife, hug the kids, promise "I'll bring you something," then head for the truck, which you started to fill with gear a full week before.

Hunters high on anticipation motor across the state, mainly from south to north, in the hours and days immediately following Thanksgiving. They fill the interstates and turnpikes with pickups, station wagons, SUVs, RVs and cars, all jam-packed with garb, gear, groceries and guns. Typically, deer hunters overpack with most extras taken along "just in case."

You can tell a camp-bound vehicle by the orange showing through back windows and on the heads of its passengers. Exiting the four lanes, scores of vehicles trickle off onto less traveled roads winding through little mountain towns, then onto other blue highways and dirt roads meandering hither and yon into whitetail country.

At the end of them, often up a rutted dirt lane lined in hemlock and beech or oak and maple, stands camp.

Sooner or later you're there, but not before a break at some standard rest stop for a sandwich and coffee, then lingering in the small, homey sporting goods store in the last town before camp. There other hunters—mainly "locals"—also gather and you lend an ear, getting updates from the local hot stove leaguers on how deer numbers have fared in the passing year.

That's the way it's done each year, and tradition is important here.

You, Sal, Wayne and Mike are the first to arrive, guaranteeing that the get-ready camp chores are yours. Someone cuts wood, another hauls it to the porch and yet another sets match to the kindling that, in minutes, yields to a warming fire.

Sal, in the meantime, draws mouse-drop patrol, vacuuming or otherwise gathering the evidence of occupancy by deer mice since the camp was last attended in an October work party.

The rest of the crew trickles in from Friday through Sunday, most of them in plenty of time to perform the ritualistic and obligatory task of sighting in rifles and checking tree stands.

Opening day for more than a half-century has been the Monday after Thanksgiving. Pennsylvania schools and factories shut their doors, taverns and restaurants open theirs and fire company and legion auxiliaries stock up on eggs, bacon, orange juice, coffee, bread, syrup and pancake batter for hunters' breakfasts.

In many areas of Pennsylvania, businesses and schools close for the week when buck season starts. The reason is simple: Everybody's out deer hunting, so what's the use?

Signs at either end of town, proclaim, "All you can eat!" and also remind customers that the doors will be open at 4 a.m. Townsfolk and travelers are the dedicated patrons. Some of the latter, perhaps camped in a nearby state park or campground, welcome someone else's role as cook ... at least at breakfast time.

You can't beat the price or the convenience. And you make a contribution to the welfare of the friendly folks who rely on the once-a-year invasion to reinforce their coffers.

Others benefit as well. Until recently, no one truly realized just how much.

Then came a study by The Center for Rural Pennsylvania. It puts things into perspective. The total economic impact of hunting in the state approaches $4.8 billion—yes, that's billion—much of it from the wallets of traveling deer hunters. You can add to that more than 45,000 jobs created by the Keystone State's hunting industry.

Even before they buy shells or ante up for gas and groceries, deer hunters must make an investment. Some 1.1 million hunters buy licenses, contributing $16.7 million per year for Pennsylvania Game Commission programs, including land purchases. Of the total, more than 70,000 licenses are bought by non-residents.

Breakfast, 5:30 a.m.: Many Pennsylvania businesses depend on the influx of dollars that hunters provide. Hunters depend on what restaurants and diners like this offer: a full stomach before a cold day in the woods.

On the eve of opening day, windows in deer camps across Pennsylvania grow amber as woodsmoke from soot-lined chimneys curls into the night sky.

The survey also shows that hunters make an estimated 7.61 million hunting trips a year, with each hunter averaging about five such outings. More than one-fourth of all such trips last 4 to 7 days; these trips are mainly for deer hunting.

It's no wonder that deer season is so important—socially, recreationally and economically—across Pennsylvania.

It's a symbiotic relationship that solidifies the relationship of the hunter and resident whose town is "invaded" every November.

And for both, it carries the promise of big bucks.

Deer camp. The words ring magic in hunters' ears. On the eve of opening day, windows in deer camps across Pennsylvania glow amber as woodsmoke from soot-lined chimneys curls into the night sky.

Deer camp is a place occupied for a only a few days each fall. Yet it holds a special spot in the minds and hearts of hunters all year long. On

The objective of all the fervor: A nice Pennsylvania buck and doe. You might see them in the open first thing Opening Morning, but after that they'll be lying real low.

the hottest days of August and the most frigid nights of February, hunters will sip iced tea or steaming coffee or something stronger, talking and dreaming of deer—and deer camps past.

I vividly recall my first deer camp experience in Sullivan County more than 40 years ago. It was where I savored my first taste of the spirit and camaraderie of the hunt. Consider it a move toward man-hood if you will. A male bonding experience as old as the hunt itself. A tentative acceptance into the clan. A ritualistic happening. And more.

For one, to be a good "deer camper" you've got to be able to take a joke. And being the new-comer to camp, the humor often comes at the youngster's expense.

Like someone hiding your hunting license the night before opening day. Sure panic.

Or taking a portrait of you perched in the outhouse. Sheer embarrassment.

Or someone sneaking into the cook's bedroom and turning his alarm clock ahead three hours.

In a Pennsylvania deer camp, as in a deer camp anywhere, you can just be who you are ... and have fun.

It happened at one Cameron County camp I know. The cook crawled from bed, dreary from too little sleep. He quietly dressed, switched on the coffee pot and began cracking eggs and pouring pancake batter. Problem was, it was only 2 a.m.

It took him and a few other groggy souls who responded to the clatter of dishes and cups several minutes to clear the cobwebs from their heads and realize that the night really hadn't slipped away so quickly.

They'd been had.

The caper wasn't fully appreciated until several months had passed. And no one's ever been sure who did it, although suspicions remain strong. Funny how time mellows such happenings. What was cursed in December becomes hilarious in July.

Of course, the essence of deer camp is the meeting of old friends and loved ones. Sons, brothers, parents, college buddies and others taken afar by jobs and marriages are brought under one roof in buck season. They come from

The essence of deer camp: being together with people who matter to you.

These old-time Pennsylvanians had a good hunt. Notice the hunting garb as well as the regenerating forest in the background. That was some good deer country.

as near as "down the road" and next door in New Jersey, Delaware, West Virginia, New York, Ohio and Maryland ... and as far as Alaska, California and Florida.

In many camps, it's as much a homecoming as a hunt. The firm handshakes. The wide smiles. Catching up on the past year.

Then comes the slow realization that the next few days won't be disturbed by ringing phones, the boss's demands, sitting in traffic or worrying about taxes. That's when the stories—truthful and otherwise—begin to flow.

Past gatherings are dusted off, polished and once again savored.

And you find yourself once again "back home" in the mountains.

Few places in the nation can boast of the rock-solid tradition of Pennsylvania deer camp. Certainly, camps of the so-called "millennium's turn" are nothing like those of the last turn of the century, when hunters hitched sleds or wagons to their mules and packed into Hammersly Fork in

wilderness Clinton County or pushed 100 miles north from Philadelphia for the solitude of Pike County's Pecks Pond.

Or they headed to any of the hundreds of other little towns and wildlands in cabin country with names like Tiadaghton, Black Moshannon, Cook Forest, Grandfather Mountain, Oil City, Cross Fork, Sinnemahoning, Hickory Run, Promised Land, Gillett, Worlds End, Germania Hill, Cherry Springs, Bucktail, Little Pine, Ricketts Glen, Tobyhanna, Hyner Run, Laurel Highlands, Kinzua, Pine Grove, the Poconos ... and the list goes on.

Today, the routes to camp are completed in a matter of hours, the interstates, turnpikes and other four-lanes providing swift access. Back then, travel time was measured in days.

Surely, none of today's deer camps are as primitive as the turn-of-the-century whitetail encampments—canvas tents, log shacks, outside woodfires, hauled water and oak meatpoles. Now sleeping bags of Holofill replace the straw- or feather-stuffed ticking which was standard issue for our great-grandfathers.

Carrying out a buck in the days before blaze orange.

I'm not old enough to have experienced deer camps of the 1920s and '30s. Few of us are. All I know is what I read about them.

But I vividly recall the more modern versions of the buckskin camps of the post-World War II era when blaze orange would have been scorned. Duck coats and plaid Woolrich suits were standard dress for the hunt, and red was the color of the day.

For the record: Woolrich, the famous central Pennsylvania manufacturer of outdoor wear and the little factory town of the same name, is today best known for high-tech clothing of Gore-Tex and Thinsulate and other materials that weren't even thought of when the first Woolrich suit was fitted to a lumberman 150 years ago. But Pennsylvanians with a sense of history will be pleased to know that Woolrich continues to offer the same classic, dark red plaids which were worn back then. The name alone brings visions of my dad and Uncle Snuffy dressed in the classic garb, heading to their stands in the Sullivan County woods.

For many hunters, the hand-me-down Woolrich coat and pants are as much as part of the hunt—cold weather permitting—as carrying Grandad's Winchester Special. Visible beneath the mandatory fluorescent orange vest, Woolrich continues to be worn by deer hunters with a sense of the past.

Some deer campers won't have it any other way.

Most hunters gained entry to a camp courtesy of a father, uncle or some special person who thought enough of them to share the experience and the mystique—and pass on the tradition.

I can still remember my first night at my dad's deer camp. I was 18 at the time and a freshman at Lock Haven State College (now University) in Clinton County. My dad hosted me for the opening day of buck season at Tall Maples Hunting Lodge in Sullivan County, about a 90-minute drive east of school. (I even managed a second day of hunting by getting lost along the Loyalsock Creek on the opener, wandering around in the dark for over four hours, and finally being found by a farmer near 10 p.m.)

As I vividly recall, the camp was alive with activity—from long-johned members making quick runs to the two-holer to cigar-munching poker players surrounding the long wooden dining table. Yet another contingent sat on or around the old, musty couch in the living room, spinning deer tales that grew taller by the year.

It was once again the eve of another opening day.

Throughout the day and well into the night, hands caringly stroked rifles new and old, polishing stocks and adding ever-so-slight coats of oil as anticipation of the most special of hunter's days loomed on the horizon. The old standards—.30-30s and .32 Remingtons or Winchester Specials or some other type of "brush

In a good deer camp, memories of yesterday are as important as anticipation of tomorrow.

The smells of bacon and fresh-brewed coffee drift up the spiraling stairs ... a peek through the window reveals a shallow, new-fallen blanket of tracking snow.

guns," many without the high-power scopes that today top deer rifles—lined a stand-up rack along the far wall, like soldiers at attention, awaiting their call.

On the eve of the opener, talk was always of past hunts and happenings that took place at camp before and after the actual hunting expeditions. "Remember when ..." preceded most stories told late into the night. Jokes and pranks flowed as easily as the Seagrams whiskey and

Ballantine beer stocked in the camp refrigerator or stashed on the side porch.

And of course, each year brought talk of a monster buck someone claimed to have caught in his headlights, crossing the road at the bottom of the lane. It was a beauty, this one, someone promised, even bigger than the behemoth Charlie missed back in '76.

Every deer camp needs a legend. But, as an old timer once explained to me, such bucks exist only until someone gives them names. Like

conscious finally relinquishes dreams of big-racked bucks and sleep comes reluctantly. More often than not it's an abrupt nap with the dreamer jarred to consciousness by the clanging of a broad-faced alarm clock.

The smells of bacon and fresh-brewed coffee drift up the spiraling stairs, speeding up the task of dressing on a morning where a peek through the window reveals a shallow, new-fallen blanket of tracking snow.

That, my friend, is the day for which deer camps and deer hunters—then and now—exist.

Left: All of a sudden, with no warning whatsoever, there they are. How could big brown deer have gotten so close, in this world of white? Below: On stand, opening morning.

Mossy Horn, Split Rack, Ol' Joe, Flat Rack or Slew Foot.

From that moment on, the old timer warned, that buck becomes a ghost. Unkillable. A legend. Whether he ever existed or not becomes unimportant. The mere thought that he might exist, and tomorrow might be the day he slinks past your treestand to wherever it is legends hide after the first shot is fired, brings added anticipation.

With it all comes an anxiety defying explanation; like an experience one seeks to savor and grasp until the stroke of midnight, when the sub-

It matters little whether it's a rustic cabin in the backwoods, a motorhome, a leaky tent lit by Coleman lanterns or a plush lodge tucked away in a mountain retreat.

The surroundings may vary but the spirits are the same.

Sleep comes slowly and then, finally, the magic morning dawns.

The smell of coffee drifts through the bedrooms, making alarm clocks unnecessary. A restless night dreaming about big-racked bucks is nipped by the "roar" of sizzling bacon in the camp kitchen.

Nervous jokes break the tension. More teasing. Checking for extra shells. Now where did I put that drag rope? I hope I need it! How many sandwiches will I need to help me survive until lunch? Anyone have some extra flashlight batteries?

Someone sets bare feet on the porch to check the sky, then offers a forecast. Nervous chatter grows as the magic hour draws near, then the cabin falls silent as hunters head to their chosen stands.

"See you down by the spring at noon," someone reminds, alluding to the standard meeting place under the hemlocks for a fire, hot tea and burnt cheese sandwiches.

You arrive at your stand long before first light and settle in, listening to the darkness. A greathorned owl hoots from somewhere in the valley.

In the gray light you nestle against a familiar tree and await the deer hunter's dawn—none so special as on opening day.

Day tints the eastern sky as a lone shot echoes off the far hill. Then another. Then, once more, all hushes to pin-drop quiet until a squirrel leaps from an oak trunk and sends an icy chill up your back.

And so goes the day.

Oh yes, every once in a while someone shoots a buck. You get the news at the meeting place at noon. Or, perhaps, you hoof it back to camp for lunch where plans are made for an afternoon deer drive.

Mid-morning, opening morning, dragging one back to camp. Just being here makes everything a success, this is icing on the cake ... and we still have a tag left. Let's hang this animal to cool and get back out there! Life is good.

Opening morning, buck and doe crossing the open in their search for a quiet, safe corner of cover.

Lunch break, and not a bad setup for it either. Does it look like one of these hunters would like to pull this heater out to his stand?

By night your tag remains intact. But there's always tomorrow. You welcome the fatigue, the strained muscles from helping Dale drag his buck from the oak stand. When you get back to camp, three other bucks already hang from the meat pole, the biggest a mountain country 6-pointer.

Life is good and you share in the handshakes, the back pats, the story and the kill, even though your tag is still intact.

Deer camp, members soon learn, means sharing both good fortune and misfortune. As for that tag you still have, well, that just means you get to keep hunting.

Yes, it is a bonus to tie your tag to a buck. But the more camps you have under your suspenders, the more you come to understand that the joy of just being at deer camp is enough. More than anything, deer camp is an escape. A celebration of deer camps past and deer camps yet to come. An initiation. A joy. A reminder of what life and good

Sharing in the success: teaming up to drag out a buck.

times and buck hunting and friends are all about.

For hundreds of thousands of Pennsylvanians, it just doesn't get any better than that.

Want to start an argument?
If so, take a stand on how deer hunting today measures up to 10, 20 or even 30 or more years ago.

Some will take the position that the good old days are long gone.

Others—and I personally belong to this school—stake claims that the "good old days" are now.

Pennsylvania deer hunting history shows that the most famous region of the state for deer, deer hunters and deer camps has long been the Golden Triangle. This vast wilderness region is roughly a triangle with points in Warren County to the west, Bradford County on the east and Centre County to the south. It's rimmed on the north by New York. And it holds more public hunting grounds than anywhere else in the commonwealth of Pennsylvania.

Deer camps here, of course, have their own identities and names, just like deer camps anywhere. And most have stories behind them.

Those I've seen over the 40-plus years in which I've deer hunted could fill a notebook: The Bucks-Only Camp. Sleepy Hollow. 8s Or Better. Inlaws & Outlaws. Itchy Pines. Dave's Delight. Pop's Place. Scarlet Oak Camp. 18-Point Camp. Lost Weekends. Henry's Doghouse. Camp Stay A While. Life O' Riley. The Liar's Den. We're Here. Camp Shoulda Got 'Em. The Hard Luck Bunch. Among the Oaks. Honey I'm Home. And my favorite: Y'all Come Back.

Not all deer clubs, of course, own their own lands, even though they may have a deer camp in some remote county. For them, leasing a neighbor's farmland and woods or heading for a public tract is mandatory. Indeed, many rustic cabins are situated on state forests lands across the state.

Annually, the 13-county Golden Triangle region once yielded more than one-fourth of the

A modern-day Pennsylvania meatpole. As with many states, Pennsylvania deer hunting's "good old days" are now.

statewide deer harvest, the remainder coming from Pennsylvania's other 56 counties. The Triangle still yields plenty of deer each season, although not as great a percentage as in days of yore: The counties with the highest kills are now in Southwest Pennsylvania. And some of the biggest bucks are today found in the farm-and-suburbs country of the Southeast.

The Pennsylvania Game Commission compiles statistics each year based on county harvests. County lines here, although subject to change, are the biologists' "deer management units."

It may go without argument that the most famous Pennsylvania "deer town" is Coudersport, county seat of Potter County, which was once a shoo-in for the highest harvests of both bucks and does each season.

Dubbed "God's Country" by folks who live there and hunters who visit—and underscored by signs leading into the cabin-rich wilderness off Route 6—Potter County continues to draw numerous hunters as do its neighboring counties McKean, Cameron, Clinton, Lycoming and Tioga. An article written in the early '50s claimed that 20,000 "new inhabitants" invaded Potter every buck season. In two Potter townships at that time, more property taxes were paid by owners of deer camps than by full-time residents.

Potter still conjures up thoughts of the ideal setting for a log cabin camp with woodsmoke scent in the air— and a deer behind every tree.

Many will argue that Potter and other north-country deer hunting opportunities have changed for the worse, the result of too many doe licenses being issued. Others counter that there are, indeed, fewer whitetails but that herds are in better balance with their limited food supplies, and therefore, in better condition. The does are getting bigger and bucks have better racks, they say.

Some indications are that fewer hunters are heading to the Golden Triangle and other mountain counties because there are better and bigger deer at home, often surprisingly close—or actually within—city and suburb.

Yet, not surprisingly, most hunters opt for deer camp. They exhibit a definite psychological need to return to the same camp and hunt the same stand of woods they hunted the year before. And the year before that. No matter if a buck was taken or not.

A study in Monroe and Potter counties in the 1950s showed that 50 percent of all deer hunters held memberships in "deer clubs" at that time. And a survey of all hunters indicated that 70 percent spent opening day in the same place for the previous five years.

I have no idea as to whether the dedication continues to hold up today, nearly a half-century later. My guess is that it does, as post-season forecasts listing areas with high deer concentrations do not draw hunters away from their familiar hunting grounds, where fewer deer are to be found.

More than two million acres of state forest, a half-

Pennsylvania's Golden Triangle offers plenty of deer. These days, bigger bucks may be had closer to home, but the allure of deer camp— really getting away from it all—brings hunters back year after year.

Hunters ... exhibit a definite psychological need to return to the same camp and hunt the same stand of woods they hunted the year before.

million acres of national forest holdings and 1.4 million acres of state gamelands tracts lure hunters to the Golden Triangle and other white-tail country camps. But not everyone holds membership in or is part of a club that owns one.

For many travelers, "deer camps" are what hunters make them. They may be the homes of relatives, motels and hotels, small rental cabins, tents, campground RVs or private farms that take in hunters for opening week.

Today, some of the biggest bucks dwell behind K-Marts or roam the farm country of the Southeast. But check the turnpike and other roadways leading to the deer camps the weekend after Thanksgiving and it quickly becomes obvious that thousands of hunters are continuing the tradition. Their chances of tagging a buck—especially a big buck—might admittedly be better had they stayed home.

But for thousands upon thousands of hunters that's secondary to being a part of something older, stronger, more meaningful and more satisfying ... a mountain country deer camp.

Considering the abundance of deer today, from forested lands through farm country and into suburbia, it's difficult to comprehend that the Pennsylvania whitetail was so scarce by the turn of the century that some people stopped hunting them.

Take, as example, the tale—as told by Mike Sajna in *Buck Fever* (University of Pittsburgh Press, 1990)—of one John M. Phillips, a Pittsburgh businessman who would go on to make a name for himself in the Keystone State's wildlife conservation annals.

When you see groups of deer like this in every other field, it's hard to believe that whitetails were ever scarce in Pennsylvania.

In the early 1900s, Phillips and a friend had made their way, at considerable time and effort, to a deer camp in the Allegheny Highlands between Ridgway and Brockway. Even today, the region offers some of the state's most primitive haunts. The story begins with the pair jumping a buck on a morning hunt.

Wrote Phillips: "About 6 inches of snow had fallen, so we tracked it all day, camped on the trail that night, followed it all the next day then rested over night at the town of Brockwayville. In the morning, we took up the trail again and succeeded in jumping and killing the buck. During all that long chase, we didn't cross another deer track. I said to my friend, 'I am done. I think I have killed the last deer in Pennsylvania.'"

Of course, it wasn't the last deer but Phillips's guess may have been surprisingly close.

Wholesale butchering of Penn's Woods had taken its toll and by the 1890s deer were rare everywhere. Stripped mountains, eroded stream banks and other lost habitat, combined with a lust for venison and buckskin, eliminated the eastern elk and reduced Pennsylvania's whitetails to an all-time low. The game commission resorted to stockings, bringing in bucks and does by railroad from New Hampshire, Maine, New Jersey, Ohio, Kentucky, Michigan and some Pennsylvania breeders. From 1906 through 1924, some 1,200 whitetails were translocated as seed stock. For 20 years doe hunting was outlawed.

In 1907 a bucks-only law was passed. That year the deer kill totaled only 300. In 1928 and again in 1938 the buck seasons were closed.

Then, for as devastating as things were, the whitetails began a rapid recovery. Clearcuts open to the sun brought lush greenery. Saplings took root and deer numbers exploded.

By 1930 more than a million whitetails—about the same number as today—again roamed the Pennsylvania countryside.

But the bounty was short-lived as a pair of back-to-back, devastating winters in the mid-1930s brought mass starvation. It also created the need for doe seasons and a new way of thinking—that does are "seed stock" and only bucks should be killed.

The lesson is one not easily digested by some hunters, even today. But gradually—with tighter controls—the deer again returned in the 1940s and more camps sprung up in whitetail country, many still serving as homes away from home for hunters and their families today.

Chopping firewood and other tasks make spring and fall camp work days absolute necessities. By mild coincidence, these workdays turn into weekends that happily seem to jibe with the trout fishing opener, spring turkey season, October days made for grouse hunting, and other assorted pleasures that also deserve attention.

No matter how far from home deer camp lay— in Warren or Clearfield, Wayne or Pike—at least two work parties per year (sometimes more) are unofficially written into every camp's bylaws. Strangely, the sessions are always scheduled a week or so after the opening of trout season and on the opening weekend of the spring gobbler season.

The same holds for the opening of the fall bow season, when another work party is convened.

"Gotta go up and help shingle the roof," a straight-faced husband tells his wife. "It's in the by-laws."

Of course, Pennsylvanians don't enjoy the privilege of Sunday hunting, which leaves Friday evening and at least a few hours on Sunday for repairing roofs, trimming trees, cleaning the shed, cutting trails and planting deer clover and replacing the hinge on the outhouse door.

Some of the older deer camps have hosted generations of hunters, who have made friends with the locals—"ridgerunners," as they're sometimes called (and call themselves).

Work party weekends tend to reinforce their relationships.

I vividly recall seeing the smile on Dad's face when he'd take a break from the work party to stop at the grocery store or the taproom in Forksville or Dushore and the owner or bartender would greet him with "Hey, Homer, how's it goin'?" while offering a firm handshake.

Deer camps, spring and summer, are more homes away from home than simple places to spend the night and eat breakfast and tend to chores. It's also a way to renew acquaintances with the "locals" in a more casual way than during the buck season.

For despite the friendships that develop over the years and a healthy respect for the "big bucks" deer hunters spend in their visits, some deer campers continue to be viewed as outsiders, albeit in a sort of half-joking, half-serious way.

"Flatlanders" is the term that describes the visitors from low-country towns and cities, although they're seldom called that to their faces.

In the fascinating little book, *Flatlanders and Ridgerunners: Folktales from the Mountains of Northern Pennsylvania*, (University of Pittsburgh Press, 1983) author James York Glimm explains the cultural need of mountain people to "create" flatlander stories.

Writes Glimm, a college professor: "A flatlander tale is a numbskull story about an arrogant outsider who meets his comeuppance at the hands of a canny ridgerunner. Anxiety is the root of these tales. People living in isolated rural regions of the hill country can feel threatened by urban values, ultra-modern culture and slick outsiders. They know their world is outdated, poor and even sometimes laughable when placed beside the wealth and power of mainstream society. They tell flatlander stories because they are good defense mechanisms, anxiety relievers and psychological equalizers."

Although not all deer clubs own both a cabin or lodge and private land, many do. This, too—the posting of such lands—does not rest well with some of the "locals." But if the visitors are friendly and considerate, the imposition is often overlooked ... except in a ridgerunner/flatlander story.

Foremost is that the ridgerunner always comes out on top.

Glimm notes that "it is important (that) locals tell these tales to each other and not to outsiders."

It's the classic private joke.

At best, they're harmless and quite effective attempts to level the playing field by taking something threatening and turning it into something harmless and silly.

One such humorous tale in Glimm's book tells of a ridgerunner hunting behind his barn during doe season when a fat doe came racing out of the woods. He took aim and killed the deer just as it leaped across a fence. As luck had it, she dropped with her front legs on one side of the fence and her back legs on the other.

Just then a flatlander came running out of the woods, looked around, and not seeing the ridgerunner standing next to the barn, hauled the deer off the fence and dressed it out.

"Well, I just set down and lit my pipe and watched," the storyteller tells his friends. "And when I saw he was about done, I just walked up, put my rope around her neck, said "Thank ye," and pulled her down to the barn."

Ridgerunners 1, Flatlanders 0.

Today, unlike the distant past, a growing number of deer camps also have females in residence. Once totally a male bastion, an increasing and welcome contingent of girls and women are now sharing in the joys of deer camp and deer hunting. Some camps, however, in their unwritten codes of behaviors and bylaws, will always be the places to which men alone escape, for at least a few days each year.

Nothing wrong with that, of course. But the family camp also has its riches. Like traditional camps, family-owned cabins also dot the state. They serve as spring turkey retreats, summer vacation sites, fall getaways and, maybe, trout camps to break the spell of winter.

One feature you'll quickly note about family camps is that they're infinitely freer of dust and better organized than most all-male getaways. Curtains hang on windows and doors and the sink and toilet bowls have been scrubbed free of

In a by-gone era, you wouldn't have seen sights like this—a female hunter—in a Pennsylvania deer camp, or a deer camp anywhere for that matter. Today it's common and, more importantly, accepted.

Children also come to deer camp now. It's a place where they can take some important steps toward adulthood.

stains. Spittoons are antique adornments rather than useful receptacles and seldom is a green, coagulated item defying identification found in the refrigerator

Credit that to the woman's touch.

Here, too, kids often get their first tastes of the spirit of deer camp. Indeed, it may be their first and sometimes only touch of an outdoors free of the deafening sounds of traffic, the puzzling lure of shopping malls, computer games, television and the thousand-and-one other diversions that today lead youngsters down frightening and troublesome paths.

At camp, the air and water is cleaner, the scenery more spectacular, the aura calmer and the diversions—like the sight of a red fox along the trail or a wild turkey greeting the morning—more healthy and exciting.

Many people today scoff at the thought of hunting being among the purest of ways to strengthen family bonds and family values.

The hunting family knows better.

Yet it is troubling to learn that the numbers of junior license buyers (ages 12 to 15) in Pennsylvania plunged from 160,000 just over a decade ago to about 100,000 today. Our ranks are aging and recruits are becoming more difficult to find. Blame it on the places they live, the demands on their time and society's push to turn kids into adults long before they're so prepared.

Outdoorsman Robert Ruark wrote that whatever is changed must be replaced with "something of value."

The family deer camp—no matter where in Penn's Woods it stands or when it is visited—surely adds something of value and memories in a child's life.

While deer camp memories are strong, details somehow blur and blend as years slip away. That's why, in the late '60s and '70s when I hunted with a dozen or so friends at Greentree Lodge on the bank of Lake Harmony in the Pennsylvania Poconos, we began a tradition that recorded the history of our deer camp happenings.

The camp log fills several scrapbooks and one year we combined past logs into a sizable volume, a history book of sorts. It shall be handed down to my sons some day.

Each camp member took turns in authoring duty across the years. And each kept detailed notes, recording what happened and when.

Who was there and who shot what?

Who bagged the biggest buck in 1971?

Who got lost in Lime Hollow?

Whose treestand was gnawed off by a porcupine?

What year was it that Ray found a porcupine in his treestand?

When was the first coyote seen in our Lehigh River hunting grounds?

Who left his license at home and had to make a 100-mile round trip on opening morning?

Included in the logbook are the details. The jokes and barbs. The camp menu. The rosters telling who was there, what guns and calibers were used, who shot deer ... and who missed, thereby losing his shirt-tail.

And there are pictures. Lots of pictures.

Such reliable references keep men honest.

When Louie starts bragging about the monster 8-pointer he shot in 1967, someone pulls out The Greentree Lodge Logbook. It shows him proudly posing with a small Y-buck.

"Oh yeah," he admits sheepishly. "Guess it grew a bit since then."

Log books are as different as the characters that give them life.

Rich are the camps whose history is told at the flip of a page.

Above: In pictures and words, a logbook captures all of a camp's memories. Below: A Pennsylvania deer stand can take on many forms, both traditional (inset) and non-traditional. Here, one hunter has solved the age-old conflict of how to be a couch potato and a deer hunter at the same time.

This meatpole will look much better in a few minutes, sagging once again under the weight of a good Pennsylvania whitetail.

As I write this, it's that time of year again. Tomorrow night the fires will burn bright, curling woodsmoke into the crisp night in a thousand and more camps across whitetail country. Monday, well before first light, the bobbing beams of flashlights will pilot orange-coated hunters to their favored and familiar stands in the forests and on the field edges.

By dusk, camp poles will hang heavy with deer. If not, talk of the day's misses and the ritual of snipping shirt-tails for those who didn't shoot straight will fill the hours, and thereafter sleep will come more easily.

But first, following supper, we'll pile into trucks and take a drive into town, at the bottom of the mountain, then stop by a few neighboring camps on a ritualistic annual visit. We'll say hello, check the meat poles and hear prolonged stories of the day's successes. It's what deer hunters do— have done for decades—and we hope will do for decades more.

I'd like to have been part of a deer camp, say, 60 or 70 years back, mainly to verify my belief that little has changed among avid deer hunters and the spirit of the camp scene during this century.

Certainly accommodations are more comfortable now and campsites are more easily attended. Explorers and Jeeps fill the front yards of the mountain camps. No longer need anyone curse

getting stuck in the snow and mud with the Old Model T, or hiking and mule-tripping into the hinterlands as our forefathers did. Four-wheel-drive Broncos and Silverados have replaced those tin relics.

Hunters dress differently too, and deer are more abundant and widespread now than when our great-grandfathers took to the forests. Variable scopes enhance shiny guns, some with plastic stocks of which my grandfather would surely make comment. The arsenal is stacked on the camp rack and the line-up of Sorels and Gore-Tex and Cordura boots next to the door underscores a modern time.

But you know the anticipation's the same as it was in those wind-blown tents of the early century. And the smells too, are much alike. Whether it's the alluring odor of Hoppes No. 9, Remington gun oil, the musky odor of a wool coat or the addictive scent of frying bacon and black coffee wafting through the camp kitchen, an escape to deer camp satisfies, stimulates and sharpens all of the senses. Dyed-in-the-Woolrich Pennsylvania deer campers wouldn't have it any other way.

It takes me back—if only through a heightened imagination—to the time of the lumberjacks, miners and hard-working townsfolk who labored above ground and under to feed their families. Then, once a year, they'd come together to play hard in the backwoods deer camps, returning home with a refreshed sense of what's important and what's not, if not somewhat fatigued by their "vacation." For those lucky or skilled—or a bit of each—venison would be the meat *du jour* for many family dinners.

Several times a year, whenever my thoughts drift to deer camps present, past and future, I'll draw the late John Madson's book, *The White-Tailed Deer* (Winchester, 1961), from my shelf and again read his poem, "Palace In The Popple," which John allowed me to include in articles written a dozen years back, with his personal blessing:

PALACE IN THE POPPLE

It's a smoky, raunchy boars' nest
With an unswept, drafty floor
And pillowticking curtains
And knife scars on the door.
The smell of a pine-knot fire
From a stovepipe that's come loose
Mingles sweetly with the bootgrease
And the Copenhagen snoose.
There are work-worn .30-30s
With battered, steel-shod stocks,
And drying lines of longjohns
And of steaming, pungent socks.
There's a table for the Bloody Four
And their game of two-card draw,
And there's deep and dreamless sleeping
On bunk ticks stuffed with straw.
Jerry and Jake stand by the stove,
Their gun talk loud and hot.
Bogie has drawn a pair of kings
And is raking in the pot.
Frank's been drafted again as cook
And is peeling some spuds for stew
While Bruce wanders by in baggy drawers
Reciting "Dan McGrew."
No where on earth is fire so warm
Nor coffee so infernal
Nor whiskers so stiff, jokes so rich
Nor hope blooming so eternal.
A man can live for a solid week
In his old underbritches
And walk like a man and spit when he wants
And scratch himself where he itches.
I tell you, boys, there's no place else
Where I'd rather be, come fall,
Where I eat like a bear and sing like a wolf
And feel like I'm bull-pine tall.
In that raunchy cabin out in the bush
In the land of the raven and loon,
With a tracking snow lying new to the ground
At the end of the Rutting Moon.

Deer camp.
May woodsmoke forever curl from its chimney.

Western
Prairies & Plains

Wyoming

Prairie Deer Camp:
Wyoming

If your hunting takes place in more traditional places—big timber, woodlots, brush, swamps, forested hills or mountains—the prairie at first seems like an odd place to be pursuing deer. But one trip Out Here and you'll change your mind—the wind, the sun, the endless sweep of hills and sage and grass and badlands marching to the horizon—this place was made for deer hunting. In the end, the prairie may give you the purest hunt of all, out there in the Wide Open, poking around the nooks and crannies and really hunting up a deer.

In this case, the deer are mule deer, and nobody knows them—or the hearts of hunters—better than **JIM VAN NORMAN.** *A real-life cowboy who works cattle most of the year, he also writes, photographs, guides, and of course hunts, right out of his Wyoming ranch.*

Get ready to escape all your worries and let your eyes feast on a horizon a hundred miles away, for you're in Wyoming now ...

Prairie Deer Camp: Wyoming
By Jim Van Norman

The alarm is set for 4:30 a.m., but I wake up about every hour, watching the clock. Then I stare at the ceiling for a few minutes, going over in my mind and making certain that I have taken care of all the preparations for the arrival of my deer hunting clients. I'll have only tomorrow morning to tie up any loose ends, as the deer hunters will be here in the afternoon.

Mule deer camp, the night before the hunt is to begin. Whether you're 8 or 80 or anywhere in between, this evening of anticipation, with all of tomorrow's possibilities, is one to savor.

Each time I awake and stare at the clock, I'm reminded of the excitement I felt as a young boy when my father would say, "Get some sleep son, we're going deer hunting in the morning!" My feet would tingle and my legs were so loaded with energy I couldn't hold them still. My mind would race with the endless possibilities that the following days might bring. Although I didn't have a clock to watch in those days, I drifted in and out of sleep, anxiously awaiting Dad's wake up call.

That same excitement is with me to this day, and another element is present as well: the anticipation of providing my deer hunters with the outdoor experience of their life!

I often wonder, in retrospect, if Dad received the same "charge" that I do now with clients, when he took me out and not only shared the knowledge he had learned on his own but the knowledge his father had passed on to him. Was a big part of his gratification the wonder on my face as I learned and watched in awe, as it is with me as I watch the faces and body language of my clients? Whether the deer hunters be seasoned veterans or youngsters just getting started, I draw as much from them as they do from me. I want their experience and mine to be exciting, fulfilling, fun and successful as possible; that is the "pulse" of this Wyoming deer camp!

On again and off again all night long, he wakes you up, ghosting in and out of your dreams: mule deer buck on the prairie.

Deer camp here is the smell of pine smoke from a stovepipe. It is the dim hue of a propane light through small windows of a rustic cabin, whose occupants are pondering the darkness outside. It is an orange spark escaping the stovepipe and wafting on the air until it vanishes against a black sky. It is that sky itself, riddled with a zillion stars. It is the deafening quiet, interrupted only by the occasional muffled voices of deer hunters anticipating the following days' events, or an owl inquiring from a big cottonwood down the creek. It is the intermittent murmur of the nearby spring.

From inside the cabin, it's the hum and crackle of the wood stove. The extended sigh of the propane light as it fills the room with a frail yellow glow. The smell of pine firewood and fresh-split kindling neatly stacked in the corner. A rifle standing alone in the corner or a bow hanging against the wall, awaiting its summons. Gear bags opened and partially revealing the necessary plunder of a deer hunter. The aroma of strong camp coffee as a wisp of steam rises like a serpent

from the boiling pot. And the heat on your backside as you stand by the stove, contemplating the coming events.

For a hunter to come to this deer camp and leave all his or her toils and troubles behind—having no need to worry about details, and simply prepare their spirit for an awesome outdoor experience—that is how this camp is structured.

What's over that ridge? Is that where I'll find a big buck mule deer? Only one way to find out: Start walking.

I've put this camp together to be a little on the primitive side. I do it purposely because there is something spiritual about coming from the hustle and bustle of big city life, or at least everyday life, and stepping back in time: existing, if only for a week, in a manner comparable to an explorer, old trapper or pioneer hunter 150 years ago.

I do this because I spent the first 15 years of my working life in high-stress positions. Being a charter pilot and flight instructor for several years, and then a commercial real estate broker for 10 more, put me on the edge of insanity more than once. The only thing that kept me from "flipping" was the time I spent in the outdoors, hunting and camping. The solitude, along with the simple existence, cleansed my mind and body and recharged my spirit. Without it, I'd have been lost to the continuous pressures of society.

Many times I went alone and many times I went with hunting partners. The times alone were the most purifying for me, but equally enjoyable was hunting and camping with good friends. Bouncing ideas and problems back and forth while staring into an evening campfire makes all the difficulties of your world seem trivial. And simply reveling in each others' hunting successes—listening and reliving the awesome natural events of each day— clears an overloaded mind.

A rancher, outfitter, writer and photographer now, I am far from entrenched in the stresses and strains, the hustle and bustle, of today's world. So I try to give my clients a little of the life I'm lucky enough to participate in every day. In this deer camp I set the stage for an opportunity to take a deer, and also for an ailing spirit to heal.

My deer hunters either rent a car in town (55 miles away) and drive to the ranch, or my guides and I go pick them up at the airport. Generally we pick them up at the airport. If they are old friends I give them a big welcome-back handshake and a hard time about something they did (that was short of brilliant) in past years. There is always much laughter and the best smiles you ever saw.

If the hunters are new to my camp I welcome them with a firm handshake and a big smile and make them feel as welcome as a person can feel on the first meeting. I politely introduce them to the old friends, if they haven't already met on the plane, as well as to my well-seasoned guides. We all talk of the past winter and summer and how I thought it affected the deer herd while awaiting their gear at the baggage claim. The question always comes up, "Are there some big ones out there this year?" My answer is always the same, with a smirk: "We'll have to see when we get there, won't we!"

My guide and I grab their gear, commenting strenuously, "What in the hell is in here?" Everyone laughs, including the new hunters, as we load the gear in the back of the truck and pile in, headed for camp.

The anticipation is evident in everyone's voice and on their face as we cover the miles to the ranch. The stories of past years fly about the cab—much to the amazement of the new hunters, whose eyes dart back and forth trying to catch every detail. It's always evident to me that they are excited but cautious, as most new hunters should be. I must pass a few more tests before they'll relax.

Above: Deer camp on the prairie, on the banks of the aptly named Cottonwood Creek. Right: Unloading gear.

Deer camp is located at the head of Cottonwood Creek, about a quarter mile above the ranch house. I picked the location because of its solitude. The location is out of the prevailing wind, has some big cottonwood trees for shade, a free-flowing spring nearby and a great view of the prairie. As we top over the hill and start down into camp some of the return hunters comment, "It's great to be back." And the new hunters generally say something like, "Man this is a neat spot!"

The therapy begins.

We pull into the circle drive, everyone unloads, then the hunters immediately begin unpacking gear bags and rifles or bows. Our cabins are set up for four people in each, so I pretty much let everyone decide on their own who they want as bunkmates. It's always amazing to me how eager the past deer hunters are to make the new folks comfortable and show them the "ropes"; when in the big city they would seldom speak to a stranger.

The guides and I make sure everyone is familiar with the lights in the cabins, the wood stoves and where to find the firewood. We point out the water for washing and drinking and the location of all the backup equipment as well as the location of the "space capsules" (two portable outhouses).

Once everything is unloaded and everyone has found a spot, I announce that I am going to go check with my wife Perri, who does the cooking for this camp, to see what time supper is planned. This gives everyone time to organize themselves a bit, get settled in and get better acquainted with the guides. I also inform everyone that I will be back in an hour, when we will test fire their equipment to make sure it made the trip all right. I have a "3D" range set up for the bowhunters and a target range for the rifle hunters.

Upon returning, everyone has their equipment out, checked and ready to make sure it's still sighted in properly. It's a great chance for me to look at everyone's equipment and comment.

By having everyone shoot their weapon I accomplish two important tasks. One: Each hunter re-establishes their confidence in their weapons and themselves. Two: I get to see how each person reacts to having a little pressure—me looking over their shoulder—and how it may effect their performance when hunting. I've learned with experience to have my hunters shoot at a bull's eye about 12 inches in diameter (this is approximately the size of a deer's vital area). Bowhunters shoot a 12-inch circle on a "3D" target and rifle hunters shoot a dirt clump 12 inches in diameter at 150 yards. Whether with bow or rifle, to have them concentrate on a smaller area would be counterproductive. We are not trying to determine if they are expert shots; we are only trying to see if they can kill a deer, given the right opportunity.

After everyone has shot a few rounds, I comment truthfully on their displayed abilities, then tell them we will "tailor" each person's hunt based on the abilities displayed and any other personal limitations expressed by each person. We then go back to camp and put the equipment away. While we pile into the vehicles to head for the ranch house, I always "kid" someone (who knows better) about how we are going to have to tie a deer up for them to kill, based on the way they shot.

One important tradition I prepare at the ranch house each year, is to have several bulletin boards displaying pictures of past clients and the deer they've taken while here. The very first place that many of my return customers go, once inside the house, is to these boards to look at their past accomplishments. The new hunters have a great time looking the bulletin boards over as well, and their eyes get very large.

The bulletin boards hang downstairs in what I call my "hunting experience room," a place I take special pride in and where I take the necessary time to visit with clients. Here I will answer any questions or tell "the story" about the various species displayed there: mule deer, whitetails, antelope, sheep, even a Kodiak bear. I think it is important to show my credibility, not only as an outfitter but as a hunter, to the people who have trusted enough to pay their money and show up, completely at my mercy. It is also important to honor all the old friends (clients)—those who return each year, as well as those who participated in this deer camp (once upon a time)—with a picture of one facet of their trip's success, for all the world to see.

We then proceed upstairs to the kitchen where I introduce my wife Perri (the culinary specialist and an experienced deer hunter to boot) to the new hunters, and reacquaint old friendships. We also take care of all the paperwork at this point, so we can get that part behind us. Supper is then served.

The guides and I sit among the hunters at the table, rather than segregate. I think it's important to make our deer hunters feel as much a part of this deer camp as possible. Many times I recite some cowboy poetry during supper, things that I've either written or picked up along the way. People seem to enjoy cowboy humor and humor in general seems to put people at ease. It is at about this point that I begin to see the new hunters, and the old friends as well, start to unwind.

Perri and Jim Van Norman—equal and hard-working partners on their Wyoming ranch.

Fresh prairie air, the pop and crackle of a good fire, a little strumming on a guitar ... formula for one of the best and most relaxing evenings you'll ever have. And to top it off, you'll be hunting in the morning!

Shortly after everyone's food has settled we return to deer camp, drop everyone off, bid them a good night and let them know what time to expect us in the morning. This gives each hunter the remainder of the evening to prepare his gear, relax and further unwind. It also gives the guides and me a chance to make last-minute preparations. Many times some of the return hunters build a fire in the central fire pit outside the cabins at this point. There are several stumps placed around the fire for anyone who wishes to sit. There's something magical about an open fire in the darkness that relaxes and calms a stressful spirit, as well as spawns tall tales of deer-hunting experiences long since past.

As with tradition, the guides and I then visit at the kitchen table, deciding on last-minute details and completing a strategy and plan for the next day. We also discuss various tactics for specific hunters based on their displayed ability and physical conditioning. We decide who will take whom, and where. Although the guides have been out and scouted on their own previously, I bring them up to date on what I've seen lately and where, by referring to the journal that I keep on deer movements and activities throughout the year. We all tip a glass of our favorite brew and celebrate the beginning of the hunt, before retiring to bed.

Again, I experience intermittent sleep. In reality, I don't know anyone who loves deer camp who sleeps well the night before the beginning

of a hunt. If there are some hunters out there who do sleep well, there is a good chance they are not right and may need to seek some professional help!

This is traditional for me. I watch the clock. Actually, I watch both clocks. One run by electricity and one run by battery, since power at the ranch house is not always reliable. Can you imagine, with the stage I've set to this point, being late for the beginning of the hunt? Not hardly! I mentally review the preparations that should already be completed, as well as the plans for the morning breakfast and all contingency plans. Last but not least, I decide where I'm going to be with the hunters I'm guiding, come first light.

Now, you're probably thinking, "Man, this guy is the one who needs help—he's way stressed!" But not me, because instead of linking stress to these preparations, I link excitement—the excitement of deer camp and the great outdoor experiences that await in the upcoming days!

The clocks seldom get an opportunity to strike 4:30 before I get up and turn them off. I head for the kitchen to start the coffee, plugging in two 30-cup percolators that shortly begin talking back and forth with an augmented rhythm. And whether you drink it or not, it's hard to beat the aroma of fresh perked coffee—an icon of all good deer camps.

I then head downstairs to wake the guides with a traditional quip like, "Are you alive?" or "Stir your stubs boys, coffee's on!" They usually answer with a mournful groan, but then spring from the beds like kids at Christmas when they suddenly remember it's Opening Day in deer camp here in Wyoming! The guides also enjoy the opportunity to provide hunters an outdoor experience they will never forget. They're anxious to prove their ability to the hunters they are guiding, as well as enjoy the sheer excitement of the hunt. They also look forward to the intrigue, always present, when dealing with nature.

Then I head back upstairs and review the list my wife has left, concerning the day's lunches. She has already made everything and put the "pieces and parts" in the refrigerator. All I need to do is take the pieces and parts and put them into the individual lunch coolers that await; add a drink and an ice pack in each and the lunches are ready to go. Each guide is responsible for his and his hunter's lunch cooler. Also, each guide then packs a large cooler with water, snacks and various soft drinks available to the hunters, free choice, of course, throughout the day. I then pour the coffee from the 30-cup percolators into a large portable coffee dispenser. Each

Lunch on the prairie. No need to ask a waiter for window or outdoor seating, or a better view, out here. Just climb a hill, pick a rock that looks about right, plop down, pop open your cooler and enjoy.

guide and I fill a thermos with coffee for the road, in case anyone wants a cup mid-morning in the field. Breakfast generally consists of rolls, bagels and cream cheese, some type of homemade banana bread or a breakfast burrito. People don't seem to eat large breakfasts like they used to, so we stopped cooking one. At this point I gather or heat this stuff in the oven as necessary.

All these preparations are made as quickly as possible, so the guides and I can sit down for our morning "cup of mud" and traditional conversation. We gather around a big country table, cups in hand, and talk of old times and past hunts, the individuals who have come and gone over the years and of course the big bucks that got away. It's our traditional time to reminisce, wake up a little more and prepare mentally for an exciting day. We wouldn't miss this special time for all the big bucks in the county!

As the clock edges toward the time we told the hunters to expect us, we review the day's plan, gather and load our "plunder" in the vehicles and head for camp. When we top the hill and start heading down into camp we can see the pale glow of the cabin lights. A spark or two escapes a stovepipe but disappears as quickly as it appeared. Everyone appears to be ready and raring to go. Some of the hunters—the ones who have been with us before—already have the lights on in the breakfast cabin and a fire built in the stove.

Everyone greets us fully clad in their hunting clothes and ready for a cup of their favorite morning beverage and something to eat. A cooler is already in the breakfast cabin with various juices and milk. We unload the coffee dispenser and breakfast "grub" and everyone files in.

Breakfast is a stand-up affair at camp—just enough to get you going.

The time spent in the breakfast cabin is some of my favorite time. The excitement and anticipation on everyone's faces is amazing. A bunch of full-grown men and women, laden with the pressures of business and of every day life, suddenly have been transformed into children. And any youngsters in the group are almost out of their body with excitement: not just because they may have an opportunity to take a deer, but because today they can release their spirit without repercussion or judgement. Today, and for the next few days, all these hunters—young, middle-aged and old alike—can enjoy the excitement of the outdoors and the wonders of nature with the pressures of everyday life completely removed. To provide that kind of transformation is the reason I continue to bring people to this deer camp.

The room is always filled with humor, jokes

Whether you're young, old or in the middle ... and no matter what your gender or walk in life ... deer camp is the great equalizer where everyone can get excited about the outdoors.

and laughter. Of tall tales about hunts "once upon a time." Of events less-than-intelligent that happened in life as well as while hunting. Everyone laughs, a good-hearted laugh, and then tells a story about themselves. My grandmother always emphasized, "For what ails your spirit, laughter is the best medicine!" A heavy dose of humor and uncontrollable laughter is necessary in any good deer camp.

A few of the hunters sit to eat and a few remain standing. Some back up against the wood stove and seem to ponder the previous story into the depths of their coffee cup. The healing continues.

I step out the front of the cabin frequently to keep a close eye on the eastern horizon where the hint of any light is our cue to get going. Once the crack of dawn breaks I assemble everyone and tell them which guide they are going with. I wish them all the best of luck, caution them about the country being rough and then sarcastically tell them: "Keep your forked end down! We don't want anyone wrong-side up!" Everyone quickly finishes their mouthful, grabs their gear and takes it to the appropriate truck. The lights are turned off in the cabins, everyone loads up with their appropriate guide, and the hunt begins.

Headlights pierce the darkness and create a narrow corridor in the landscape, here and there, as we bounce up a two-track trail. Rabbits dart into the road and run blindly about. Dawn's blue twilight begins to sneak up on the darkness, starting in the eastern sky. Objects, beyond the truck a few yards, begin to take a vague shape as we pass. Some wispy little clouds far above the horizon begin to take on an orange or pink hue. Before long we are out of the pickup truck and perched in nature's amphitheater with a panoramic view of the countryside and the staging sunrise.

Sunrise! Another of a deer camp's icons. Witnessing sunrise is a necessary assignment for all the participants in this deer camp. Not that I give anyone a choice or chance to decline this opportunity; I make sure everyone is out sitting in the "native bleachers" awaiting mother nature

Dawn on the prairie, in a sky larger than you could ever have imagined.

to exhibit her wares. Sunrise signals the unfolding and potential of a great outdoor experience. It also cleanses the weary soul as it washes away the darkness.

An older mule deer—one 6 or 7 years old—has developed a level of intelligence far above that of the average younger mule deer buck. Having survived several hunting seasons, a cagey old mule deer buck knows the ropes very well. When he begins to notice more activity than normal every year as hunting season approaches, he immediately goes into hiding—moving to a safer part of the country and disappearing from his normal hangouts. In fact, he acts a lot like his big white-tailed cousin and becomes almost totally nocturnal after being pursued, waiting until dark before coming out to feed and heading back to a bedding sites well before sunrise.

A big buck mule deer will even limit his feeding to a very small area, so as to stay close to all escape routes and favorite hiding spots. Bedding sites are picked strategically, allowing either a panoramic view or retreating entirely to the dark timber, tangled brush and deep canyons to be totally obscured.

Many big mule deer bucks choose to live alone. I'm certain that these types of bucks want no other deer around that could potentially give away their position. In the old days these singular and spectacular bucks were referred to as "ridge-runners." Many of these old loners pick some of the highest ridges for bedding sites, where the view is endless. At the first tiny hint of trouble, they will exit to their favorite hiding spot or pick another site high on another ridge. I've seen many of these "old timers" with a few companions early in the year, but later they always break off from the bunch to go the hunting season "solo."

Another reason big mule deer are tough to hunt is their unpredictability. Sometimes, when spooked, a buck will go to the next ridge and quickly bed down and watch his back trail, checking diligently for any pursuit. The next time you "bump" him, he will dive into the thickest timber around and disappear. Or, he will bust and run to be seen sky—lining three ridges away—still on the run! You can seldom pattern a mule deer—not in how they will choose to escape, not even in their daily routines!

Add to that the muley's ability to detect movement visually, hear the slightest decibel of sound, and smell with a nose that takes a second seat to none—and a mule deer buck becomes as tough to find and successfully take as any four legged critter there is.

A mule deer buck is also beautiful to behold ... if you can find him and get a look. With a stark white muzzle on a background of deep gray, accented in black, along with a heavy and dark rack, a mule deer buck is at once well dressed, noble and proud. His big, blocky muscular body carries him well, even in huge soaring bounds, straight up the side of the most difficult terrain. A big, wide-racked mule deer sky-lining as he tops out into the next drainage is an awesome spectacle—one that will beckon your return to mule deer country, year after year.

The prairie terrain here in central Wyoming is rough and unforgiving, and that's all the better for big mule deer. Big canyons and rough breaks provide the cover and protection necessary to hold the more

A good, mature buck mule deer is stunning to behold—large blocky body, big rack, huge ears, grayer-than-gray coat, white face and black muzzle. And he is smart too—as capable as his whitetail cousin at evading you, even out here on the wide open prairie.

wary deer. Deep washes, scattered rock outcroppings and cedar thickets provide shade that mule deer prefer. Although I've seen some dandy bucks out in the sage brush flats, on the average (excluding the rut) you will find the biggest, smartest bucks in the toughest country around.

Not long after the light is sufficient to just make out images, I whisper from under my binocular-covered eyes, "There's two big bucks right over there." My hunters exclaim, "Where? Where?" I usually have to quiet their exuberance to a whisper so the bucks won't hear us. Then I give the hunters a detailed explanation of where to look.

That explanation often goes like this: "Okay. Do you see that big rock over there on that hogback? Put your binoculars on it. From there come down that ridge, to the right to that old dead tree. Then drop straight down from the tree about 50 yards to that chalky little cut bank. The deer are feeding just to the left of there." When they spot the two bucks, they are like kids in a candy store. To see that kind of animation on the bodies and faces of grown men and women, and especially youngsters, is worth a ton of gold. Their inner spirits begin to show. It's funny because when some realize I'm focused on their exuberance they get a little embarrassed and

quickly try to regain control. But they can't keep it under wraps for long and that's the way it is meant to be here in this Wyoming deer camp.

We look the bucks over carefully and determine if they are worth going after. Our goal in this camp, when it comes to harvest, is to take only mature bucks in the 6- to 7-year-old range and let the younger deer get some age on them. For the most part a buck of 6 or 7 years, around here anyway, sports an impressive set of antlers. Upon determining that one of the bucks appears to be a "whopper," we decide to attempt a stalk. Tradition calls for me to flip a coin to see who is going to try for the first buck. Or, if one person elects to pass, the other person is "up." This process is exciting in itself. Usually the shooter goes with me, and the other person stays in place to watch the action.

The stalk! There are few things more gratifying in mule deer hunting than the stalk. Whether the stalk ends with a deer being taken or not, every stalk is a success in this camp because, with each stalk, we receive some additional education about ourselves, the critters we hunt, the wonders of nature along the way, and the level of our ability. These all create the essence of hunting.

When a stalk is blown in this camp—even if it was the biggest buck around—each participant is encouraged to bask in the experience as you watch the buck clear the far ridge, laugh while thanking him for the education and assure him you won't make the same mistake again. Those who are stressed by such experiences are hunting for the wrong reasons. Sure, stalking can be a bit frustrating at times. But here in this deer camp I help folks link success, laughter and excitement to the experience of a blown stalk, in place of frustration.

Mule deer hunting is a bit different than the types of deer hunting most vistors to my camp are used to. Whitetail tactics—namely, taking a stand—are seldom used here.

This is big country, and it takes some effort and boot leather to find a good buck in all of it. He won't just stand out there in broad daylight and wait for you to shoot him. You have to get out there and look and hunt.

The key to taking a mule deer in this wide-open country is this simple idea: spotting the deer before he spots you. The best explanation of this technique is simple in theory but hard to do unless you commit yourself and work hard. What is this secret? Stay out of sight of the country you are hunting, except to belly up and peek over the edge and glass, from time to time. The places to look when glassing are primarily the shady places.

The number one place to find mule deer bucks, whether they are up and feeding or bedded down, is in the shade. Any thing or place that produces shade is deserving of your careful scrutiny.

I tell my hunters, don't concern yourself with spotting the whole deer. Learn to look for what I call "pieces and parts." Generally you will only spot a portion of a mule deer—an antler, leg, rump, face, antler, ear or other part. Concentrate only on parts of mule deer and you will find many more bucks than if you're concentrating on finding an entire deer's image.

Once we have found a deer of our choice, the challenge is to stalk within range of the hunter's firearm for a shot, or get even closer with archery gear and wait until the buck comes out of hiding. Sounds easy? Not hardly! Stalking in open country is a talent in itself. And waiting for a big buck to

stand up and stretch, or emerge from a thick bedding area, takes an immense amount of determination.

This type of approach can be an all-day proposition. It requires little movement as well as a favorable, consistent wind. Generally, "staking out" a mule deer like this, at the end of a stalk, is the best way to assure yourself of a good shot no matter what weapon you're carrying. I reinforce this on my clients, and tell them they must have fortitude!

The stalk itself takes planning too, including: identifying checkpoints along your route (making certain there is no confusion as to the deer's location); careful foot placement; proper wind evaluation (big muleys trust their lives to their noses); and a constant vigil for other deer—deer you didn't see along your stalk route when you glassed and planned.

Another important consideration—can you stalk totally obscured from view? We always evaluate this before moving on an animal. A mule deer's peripheral vision is astounding, and one of the biggest mistakes people make while stalking with rifle or bow is trying to keep an eye on the deer as they stalk.

It needn't be that way. You know the deer's basic location, so stay out of sight until you get into position for the shot. It's okay to monitor, a "bit," the area around the deer when you stop to rest during the stalk. But don't get caught "sneaking a peek" and blow an opportunity.

And last but not least, is your final destination—the place where you will wait with bow or rifle in hand for a shot to develop—within your and your equipment's effective range?

When bowhunting, the most effective way to take a mule deer buck, at the end of a stalk, is to get into position fifteen to twenty yards from the deer you've chosen and wait for a shot to develop. Forcing a deer to do something to present a shot only serves to alert the deer to your location, and it will certainly put the buck on alert. No matter how long it takes, this is the best way to get a good shot at an unsuspecting mule deer buck.

When rifle hunting, the biggest mistake a hunter can make is to hurry the shot. Generally, there is no hurry at all! In most instances the deer doesn't know there is anyone in the country. I encourage all my clients, as they move into position, to take their time, concentrate on the deer's body (not the antlers), wait for the buck to present a good shot and slowly squeeze the trigger.

As we make our way toward a buck, special care is taken to note the wind and footing. I take the time during each stalk to point out any natural wonders along the way. Like a bunch of wildflowers growing in the crack of a shear rock face. Or swallow homes perched precariously on the underside of an overhang. Or the track of a bobcat imprinted perfectly in the sand. Seldom does anything need be said, only silently pointing and simply observing for a moment is enough.

As the final distance closes, our primitive instincts begin to surface. Creeping quietly into another being's "space" without being detected is, I believe, genetically encoded in all humans. There's something magical about it. Even as a kid playing hide and seek or sneaking up on a friend to scare the wits out of them, was—and still is—exhilarating. Our eyes narrow and our senses become amazingly acute. We become motionless

I encourage all my clients, as they move into position, to take their time, concentrate on the deer's body (not the antlers) ...

and silent. Our heads crane downward and our bodies crouch slightly, as if ready to spring. Adrenaline flows and excitement wells up inside. It's an instinct that has been with us since the beginning of time and one that will be with us until the end.

Stalking for the purpose of a kill possesses all of the above elements, with an additional dose of adrenaline added. That additional surge of adrenaline again is not in anticipation of enjoying the act of killing, but rather the result of our intense

desire to succeed in all our human endeavors—to complete each effort we attempt—to society's perfection.

Unfortunately, until this goal has been reached—successfully taking a deer—the hunter never truly begins to rest. There's an unwritten pressure that exists via the presence of other hunters in camp, the expectations of those waiting at home and the need to be successful. Therefore, I never see the resolve on the hunters' faces or in their body language until after the deer is dressed and been loaded in the truck. Then, they actually breathe a sigh of "release" and the pressure is off! Then and only then, does the hunter begin to reflect on the details of the experience and absorb themselves in what hunting is really about: resting our spirit, connecting with our fellow man and observing nature's wonders.

Sure, success is among the many reasons deer camp is so necessary for many. But in this deer camp we strive to reach this understanding: that while hunting, there are no failures and success comes in many ways. Each individual decides how to measure success.

We should be turned loose from the pressures associated with society's definitions of success, where generally we are bombarded with our shortcomings and no matter our position or status in life, others tend to concentrate on our failings instead of our accomplishments.

So the opportunity to participate in the management of a wondrous natural resource plays an important part, but the act of killing and "showing it off" is not the primary motivation for hunting, nor should it be paramount in a "true" hunters mind!

Deer camp takes us to that place where we need to be, independent of all others' judgement. Into a different world, filled with natural beauty and not mortal imperfection. And by virtue of just being there, failure is averted. In the many facets of deer camp we can push ourselves to our own physical, mental and spiritual limits and be influenced only by the ethics from within ourselves, of our god and of nature.

Mule deer bucks can be taken with bow-and-arrow too (left). The keys are to look for a bedded buck in a shady spot (usually made by terrain because there aren't many trees out here), stalk close quietly and with the wind coming from the deer to you, then wait-wait-wait for him to stand up on his own. Then, if your hands aren't shaking too much or if you have enough strength left in your knees, maybe you'll make the shot. Below: High-racked buck doing the high jump.

When it becomes necessary to further prove the level of our ability, validation of success takes place when the results of our hunting efforts are presented—or folklore is born—for review by our elders, peers and descendants. This validation holds more urgency to a hunter in the early stages of individual hunter evolution than it does as the seasons pass. But make no mistake. Even to us evolving "old hunters," self validation and a nod from our peers—whether we take a deer or not—forever remains significant.

A big buck mule deer is a professional at the game of hide and seek and a wizard at detecting anything stalking him or he wouldn't have lived to be six or seven. To have the ability to maneuver to within easy striking distance, is quite an accomplishment.

As the gun barrel eases through the weeds into position or the bow is brought to full draw, this effort is a success. Regardless of the outcome, whether the deer makes good his escape or is downed awaiting our arrival, success has been attained to an impressive degree and the hunter is congratulated for his or her effort. That's the way it is in this deer camp!

If the hunter misses, we talk of the highlights of the stalk and excitement of observing the deer so close. We talk about the mechanics of the miss and laugh about controlling adrenaline. And then we revel in the prospects of having another opportunity to stalk. If the hunter downs the deer, I shake his or her hand firmly for having reached one of their goals. We excitedly proceed to the deer's location.

Considerable time is taken as we admire the deer, both the antlers and the beauty of the entire animal. We respectfully wash the deer of any external blood and take many photographs. Photographs are encouraged, not to be used for bragging rights, but as cues for our minds ... of the memories and the many facets of the overall experience, for years to come.

Happy faces like this (above and right) say it all: Mule deer camp was a success; I got a nice deer as a bonus; when can I come back?

Once back at the ranch house we take the deer from the back of the pickup and take two Polaroid pictures: one for the hunter to stick in his pocket and one for the fabled "bulletin board" in the house. Generally, we arrive back at the ranch house toward evening about the same time all the other guides and hunters are coming in. Everyone admires the deer taken and congratulates the appropriate hunter for having reached one of his or her goals. Such jubilance gives birth to "tall tales" spun of the day's action.

At supper, everyone shares the tale of their day. There is always a lot of "wows," good-hearted joking and laughter for the follies that accompany a great day of hunting. After supper we load up and drive the hunters back to camp. Everyone is then invited to sit

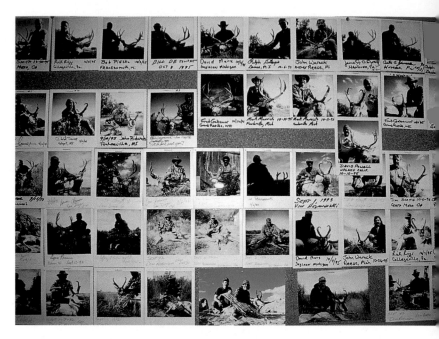

Bulletin board filled with the game and smiling faces of many successful hunts.

Sunset back at camp. Will you sleep tonight? That's a foregone conclusion after a day of sage-perfumed wind, bright sun, blue skies, walking, stalking, and heart-thumping excitement on the Wyoming prairie.

and talk around a roaring fire and drink their favorite "toddy." (Two is the limit so no one gets too loose!) But the time around the fire seems to be the time that all guards are finally let down, friendships are deepened and new connections are made. A time when the spirit truly begins to rest.

Some may say this camp sounds too serious, but serious we seldom are. The concepts offered here only enhance the amount of fun that everyone can have. And as I sit and listen each year, while the flames dance methodically, knowing the sun has set on another fine day of hunting, I hope ... that the sun never sets on the vision and memories provided in this Wyoming deer camp!

Heartland Farms

Wisconsin

Going Home: Wisconsin Whitetails

While the traditional deer camp involves travel and adventure to get there, many of us can hunt right from our homes, driving each day to our hunting grounds. Fortunate enough to live in good deer country, we eat at our own table, sleep in our own bed. Home becomes a deer camp of the mind, a time of year made different and special because it's deer season and there are hunters in the house.

TOM CARPENTER writes of such a place — a Wisconsin home he returns to each year, to hunt the same woodlots, fencelines, creekbottoms and farm fields he did as a boy. He talks of going home, the people, the land ... and of trying somehow to recapture, in a busy life of this day and age, some of the simple joys of just deer hunting.

You're going to farm country now, and it could be any of a number of places in our nation's heartland where deer can still run and hunters can still hunt ...

Going Home: Wisconsin Whitetails
By Tom Carpenter

I could start at the beginning and tell you about being a boy in a small town nestled among southwestern Wisconsin's rolling hills of farmland and woodlots. You'd hear about November: that most glorious of months when, from my family's home on the edge of town, I could watch the hills turn from tan-and-green to brown and then shades of gray as the corn harvest came in, the long nights froze the luster out of the hayfields, and the woodlots—save for the oaks—lost the rest of October's leaves.

I'd talk about what November meant to someone whose earliest memories are of my father coming home from hunting with a game vest full of squirrels. I'd pull them out one by one, out in the garage, and smell their forest aroma, imagining that I had been out there hunting with my dad, my back against an oak or hickory, watching the sun go down and just being there.

Time drags on forever when you're young and have plenty of it, but of course the day finally came when I did get to hunt squirrels (the game of September and early October) as well as rabbits and pheasants (the game of late October and early November). But there was always something bigger and even more exciting looming on the horizon every autumn, as those hills made their journey towards winter.

That something bigger was the Saturday before Thanksgiving—deer season. No ordinary nine days, mind you, but Deer Season. A small town in southern Wisconsin deer country changes then, for families like mine—which was most of us—who couldn't afford to, didn't have time to or didn't see a need to run up to the fabled northwoods or even the storied deer forests of the central parts of the state. There was adventure in the hills and woodlots, deer, and some wild places if you were willing to walk a bit and look carefully.

I would tell you about the sunny, frozen Saturday morning when my father and brothers brought home their first deer, describing the excitement I felt—riding my bike down the street and seeing the car in the driveway, so early in the day they must have gotten something. Rugs and a little blood adorned the

Cornfields, hayfields,
brushy fencerows,
grassy swales,
woodlots, haybales on
the ridge ... the arena
for a Green County,
Wisconsin, farmland
deer hunt.

Father and older brothers, first deer, 1972. The old apple tree helped cool out a few more deer until meeting its demise one year in a big wind.

trunk where I knew they had carried the deer home, and I ran around to our backyard. We hung the deer in the old apple tree in the back corner.

Home was deer camp—still is—a time and state of mind as important as any deer camp anywhere.

A Wisconsin deer season was big then, especially when I finally got to rise early with my older brothers and my father to hunt. And it's big now, even though I've since moved far away and grown a crop of responsibilities that carry my worries far beyond those few I had when I wandered those Green County hills at will. But I return each year to that house on 12th Avenue on the south edge of town and then to a couple farms only a few miles away, where a piece of my heart resides year 'round, there among the oaks and creekbottoms and hayfields.

Yes, I could start at the beginning. But in many ways, deer hunting—deer "camp," being home and hunting in the hills of Cadiz Township—means more now than it ever could have then. Maybe it's because I know now that I won't be here forever. Maybe it's because I also know that those I love, and love to hunt with, will not be here forever. Maybe it's because I finally realize what a blessing this wild corner we hunt really is—in a landscape being tamed more and more each year with the spread of development and "progress." There are a lot of reasons *why*.

Headlights sweep across bare tree trunks as I swing the old truck into my garage. A bushel of cottonwood and oak leaves rattle in behind me, pulled by the truck's draft and pushed by the November breeze. 10:30 p.m. A family sleeps inside the house, and a bed awaits me too, but not yet.

I sit for awhile and think about the immensity of everything: The vehicle in the stall next to me, used to haul children around, that still needs payments. Three kids who need to be fed and clothed and raised and helped, if I can at all swing it, with college. The house that always needs

Buckhorn Road seems a good name for a place to hunt deer.

payments. An endless parade of projects and fix-ups and dishes and laundry and whatnot for my wife and me, and snow shoveling in winter and lawn mowing in summer. The stack of work on the worn seat beside me. The stories that need writing. The paperwork and bills on my desk inside.

I could get out and sweep the leaves back into the night, but they remind me of where I am going tomorrow and I sort of like them for that reason. So I sit another minute, in the quiet, not immobilized by all of it but thinking deeply and peacefully about how it's all going to have to stand still for awhile. For tomorrow I travel to Wisconsin, driving the length of the state, pretty much north to south, in this old truck, to my boyhood home and where, along Buckhorn Road in the rolling hills of Green County's Cadiz Township, deer season will open the day after that.

So I step out and remember to close the garage door, smelling November in the Minnesota air and shuddering a bit at the chill and feeling a little better about everything, reminding myself to throw in some extra wool socks as I head inside to start packing.

It always seems odd—this gathering together of gear to go to a place I once called home, to hunt. But the fact is that I, like so many other children of the Midwest's rural areas and small towns, have ended up in bigger towns or metropolitan areas to, as I put it, find some economy. Children of the 1950s and '60s, we left in the '70s and '80s to find jobs, to make our way in the world, whether we had roots we cared about or not back home. There was not enough there for all us, so we headed out for opportunity.

And even though I hunt in many places now, a Wisconsin deer season, looming there at the merging of fall and winter, produces a sweet anticipation the same way it did over a quarter century ago. That's a long time, I think, lugging gear up the stairs and out into the garage at midnight.

But I will return again, as I always do, having never missed a season in all that time since my first when I was 12 years old—because I love being there, love hunting with my father, who is past 80 now and still hunting, and I love the country.

I think about my brothers who don't make it back to hunt any more, and wonder if they too are recalling those days of old when deer hunting brought us all together. Looking back on those days, those precious few days when we were all at home together or at least they were returning from college to hunt at home, I'm always sad to

Above, from left: Snapshots, from the archives of a deer-hunting family. The old photo albums of any deer-hunting household in rural Wisconsin, Minnesota, Iowa, Illinois, or anywhere else in the Heartland, will harbor a similar display.

find those times fading a little bit from my memory each year.

But I like to believe that, in spirit anyway, this hunt does bring some of those memories back a little stronger, keeping that flame alive inside me, and them.

As always I am alone on a pilgrimage of sorts now, this day before the Opener, driving the length of Wisconsin and anticipating the Big Day to come. The countryside passes mile-by-mile, and it is good to see it all—the woods, the fields, the farms, the marshes—and know there is still so much of it out there, where deer can still roam and hunters can still hunt.

As the sun begins its afternoon descent and I near the state's southern counties, the traffic is very heavy in the freeway's northbound lanes—hunters from Madison and the southeastern cities, heading Up North. I don't feel jealous of them or their adventures up in the Big Woods. For by now I have one place in mind—300 acres of hay- and cornfields, creekbottom marsh, hills, oak woodlots and fallow pastures my father and I are fortunate enough to have access to, in Green County's Cadiz Township, not far from the Illinois line.

It is here that we have hunted since I can remember. Oh, we made brief forays into Lafayette County when my Uncle Alvin was still alive, to hunt with him, and even spent a few years hunting in Iowa

As the roads traveled change from freeway to highway to county road to township road, so do the towns go from big to tiny ... and you start feeling better and better. The valley of the Pecatonica River cradles Browntown, right where Skinner Creek flows in.

County where you can use a rifle. We had but one rifle, and traded off using it, everyone else in our family hunting group using shotguns and slugs. But this particular destination—just "Browntown" or the "Sandplant" we call it— is where our hearts have always been, and it is here that I will stop, even before I go to my parents' home in town.

I park on some high hill to watch the sun set, maybe seeing a deer and maybe not, but just feeling good to be here once again. It's always a relief to see that "our" woodlots are still safe from the incessant housing developments and subdivisions and single homes that are creeping into more and more of Southwestern Wisconsin's wilder spots each year, making them unfit for deer hunting (especially gun hunting, such a rite in this state) and taking away the character of this lovely, hilly rural land. I have no control over any of that, but I nevertheless say a prayer that this particular section of land will stay safe a few more years. It's all I can do, not owning any of it or even living here any more.

So I stop here at this bit of deer-hunting paradise—to smell the earth, hear the wind and see the sun peek between a cloud bank and the horizon, spreading its yellow-orange glow over this valley of the Pecatonica River. I can see it in the distance, tree-lined and winding slow and dark and muddy through the riverbottom corn stubble, as I zip up my jacket against the cold.

You can tell it's deer season, here in Green County, just by driving a few miles in the countryside—even through town—even if you're not a hunter:

► A few more cars are gathered at the farmhouses—family or guests home for deer hunting.

► Orange hangs on clotheslines, in respectable attempts to air out the smells accumulated during a year of storage in the basement or attic.

► A tavern behind the railroad tracks displays a red "Deer Registration Station" sign next to Badger and Packer slogans (two other pastimes that almost approach deer hunting as a Wisconsin religion).

► And, after about 10:00 a.m. tomorrow, deer—bucks and does, big and small and every size in between—will hang from backyard trees, or travel here to there in the beds of pick-ups or even in the trunks of sedans, their legs sticking out and surely their heads too if they have antlers.

► And tomorrow night my mother will invariably report on the shots she hears from the backyard when she went out to water the dog—the "boom-boom-boom" volleys you wouldn't hear from pheasant or rabbit loads but you do from slugs in the nearby countryside.

One of the rites of Wisconsin deer hunting is the registration station—where deer are checked in, every tailgate and trailer and truck bed and trunk is examined by everyone else, and just plain hunting tales start their growth curve to becoming tall tales.

This is Wisconsin. This is Deer Season. Even some schools and businesses will close down for the week. Certainly the state-of-mind is different than the rest of the year, and very special to the state's 600,000 hunting residents—and a few native sons like me that return each year to relive the tradition. For many of them, home is deer camp.

And then I am home.

The evening before Opening Day is always time of bittersweet anticipation.

On the sweet side, I am here, with my father, who is now past 80, and we are going hunting together again. Possibilities are endless on this night of all nights—better than Christmas and your birthday and New Year's Eve all rolled into one—and spirits are high, for tomorrow is The Day and we can feel it. Oh, we will hunt for several more days after that, but Opening Day is just the time when most deer are bagged.

On the other side of that anticipation—deep down we are always wondering how many more deer seasons will we have together. And we also recall, though it is in our own minds and we dare not say it out loud because we are men—those glorious days when my brothers and I were young: the chaos of three teenage boys gathering gear and making sandwiches and getting ready for The Day and loading the trunk of our family sedan under frigid starlight in the black night, knowing we'd be back out in it again before the sun rose.

In this house, and thousands like it across Wisconsin, lights will be on hours before dawn in the morning. The hunters inside will be dressing and trying to gobble some breakfast and making coffee and then rushing out the door to follow the headlight parade out of town; you'll see some blaze orange in all the vehicles as they turn off the highway here and there to wind their way down the backroads to a farm they have some access to.

Eve of the opener, gear piled high at the door, ready to go before dawn in a few short hours.

what escape routes they are using—as they move from woodlot to creek-bottom, marsh grass to woods, fence-line to brush patch, here to there or there to here, anywhere. Each year seems to have its own special set of movement patterns. So we usually end up shifting our stand locations by mid-morning—or altering our strat-egy altogether for awhile and basing our location shift on what we have seen happening and what deer we have seen moving about the country-side—to try and get a deer.

When needed, we will do little "pushes" of our own, another kind of Plan B, to try and move some-thing into our sights.

And so we hunt.

I have perfected the technique of maximizing our hunting time with minimal exertion. Used to be that, like everyone else, we trudged back to our vehicle for coffee, snacks or lunch or a rest, wasting valuable hunting time in the process.

My father is not a fast mover. For that matter, I am not either anymore. So here's what we do.

When we arrive at the farm and hunting grounds, well before sun-up, I will drive on a tractor trail through a field toward our chosen spot, headlamps out, and drop off my father in the dark. This saves him the long walk in, and he will be fresher for the day; he will take a stool to sit on. I then drive out to the farmyard, park, and walk back to the woods and fields, carrying two packs—one with any gear and extra clothes we might need, the other filled to bursting with thermoses, pop, water and food for the day.

This way, no matter what we are doing—and we do a lot of just standing around on some wood-lot edge, drinking coffee or hot chocolate, eating sandwiches and visiting—we are hunting. And you'd be surprised how many deer we get, just being out there and not sitting in a vehicle at road-side or watching hay bales or cows in the barnyard.

The preparations are much quieter now. So we just pack and plan and draw maps we don't need to draw because we have hunted these hills and woods and fencelines and fields for so long. We strategize on where the deer might be feeding (cut corn), where they'll be bedding (the same places they have for over 25 years, shifting occa-sionally as dictated by changes in the land and its use) and where we might sit to intercept them as they travel to evade neighboring hunters.

You might see a deer moving naturally from feeding to bedding grounds, or even catch a buck out rutting, on Opening Morning. But it doesn't take long for bucks and does alike to learn the les-son that something is amiss in the countryside, and after that they will lie awfully low. So low you might not think there are any deer around at all.

We always end up taking a stand in one of a half dozen or more standard spots, to wile away the first few hours of the day. These spots are always well-thought-out, but they seldom pro-duce. We do shoot deer, but it's usually on a Plan B and not on this Opening Morning Plan A. Here's why, I think.

This is fairly open country, and you can see what's going on—where the deer are traveling,

Above: Those who aren't foolish might eat venison throughout a Wisconsin winter. If you've got an antlerless permit and are going to use it, take your first good opportunity because you very well might not get another chance like this, even if the season is only an hour old.

Any deer is a good deer in Cadiz Township, in our book. Of course, everyone wants a buck. But the reality is this—there are good numbers of deer here, but bucks are hard to come by. In fact, any deer is by no means easy to get, and if you don't take advantage of your first opportunity, or you decide to wait for a buck when you have a "hunter's choice" or antlerless-only permit in your pocket, you could very well go without venison that winter.

Of course, you only shoot a "Big Doe" if you do decide to take an antlerless deer. You never hear someone at the check station or in a tavern after the hunt say "Yeah, I got a real little doe out by South Wayne" or something.

A buck is a bonus: any buck, because Quality Deer Management has not yet come to Cadiz Township. And that's all right, because to me the bucks we do get, on occasion, are the best quality anywhere, anyway: stocky, thick-antlered deer from spikes to 8-pointers but mostly 5s and 7s and other oddities like that (we've never gotten one bigger than 8 points)—just Cadiz Township bucks that are blocky, thick and fat. An ax-handle wide across the ass, as Dad would say.

This is not trophy hunting. This is just deer hunting—for the joy of it, for the companionship, for being out in the Cadiz Township hills in November—smelling the earth and the air and cleaning out your mind, and for getting a whitetail if you're persistent, lucky, fortunate or good.

Occasionally the stars all line up perfectly and one of us shoots a deer off their Opening Morning stand. This is the exception rather than the rule, because most kills come under one of the Plan B scenarios, after Opening Morning's barrage has tapered off and we're wondering where all the deer are this year. One particular deer though, a buck, stands out as an opening morning, an opening minute, success.

It was the autumn after I had left home for good. But I promised myself, come hell or high water, that I would be back for deer season. And so I was—reaching the Wisconsin border at 7 p.m. after working all day and half the night before to get an extra day off on the other side of the weekend, home by 12:30 a.m. Now it is 6:00 a.m., my father and I sitting in his station wagon waiting for a little light.

We walk down through the farmyard in that gray murk between starless night and cloudy day, a few snowflakes drifting down. I take a stand at the best place I know, having not been here for almost six months, leaning up against a huge and old white oak. I am in The Nursery—a brushy, steep, rocky gully that once held an old sandbox and tire swing as a playground for some long-forgotten landowner's children.

Model T and Walnut Tree in The Nursery. It makes a good deer blind if you've got a north or south breeze blowing.

Deer like to hang out here—it is now a brushy tangle of berry bushes and brambles among a few old oaks and hickories. The deer hesitate and skulk in the area a bit before exiting into the fields and taking a run up a fenceline to the next woodlot, The Nob. For many years there was an old, rusted Model T here—a walnut tree growing straight up through where its engine and hood should have been.

I hear them coming in the dusky dawn, almost imperceptible crunches in the leaves on the sidehill above me, way before shooting light. But the deer are in no rush—I wonder if they really are deer or if it is my imagination—and my ears struggle to hear the occasional hoof fall in the tick-tick-ticking of the falling snow.

*And then,
finally, there
he is. Head
up, antlers
poking straight
into the
gray sky ...*

And then, finally, there he is. Head up, antlers poking straight into the gray sky—a buck—standing 50 yards away, in a clearing. Two or three does peek out from the woods, but my eyes are riveted on him. At my shot—I can see fire coming from the barrel but it truly is two minutes into legal shooting time—he sprawls out, then takes off and is gone.

I walk over, hop the barbed wire fence with my hands shaking, and find sprays of crimson, quickly turning pink as the now-big flakes begin to cover the blood. I follow the color—it's exhilarating and a bit scary at the same time—worrying that the buck has gone a long

way and I will have trouble recovering him. Then the tracks turn toward the brushy fenceline I am paralleling and I look up and there he lies: a 7-pointer stretched out on the foxtail and goldenrod, one antler resting against a wooden fence post.

By the time I have him dressed and am dragging him back toward my stand, the alfalfa stubble is covered, the ground is white and he slides easily over the snow—still warm and flexible and not yet stiff as he glides over the dips and swales, behind me. I have to detour around a big round hay bale.

More often than not though, the deer we get are shot under a Plan B. The best of these options, one we use sparingly, is the one-man "push." The idea is not to go busting through the brush, but to stalk or still-hunt slowly through good cover—usually a small, out-of-the-way spot—while one partner waits at a likely crossing, hoping to intercept any buck or doe sneaking away. This works often enough to keep us trying it.

It's not really a "drive" as much as it is a "sneak" or "push." These whitetails, like deer anywhere, go where they want to go and not where you want them to go. Your best strategy is to know a likely escape route—whether it's directly away from the area you're pushing or to the side or maybe even behind it and often in a different piece of cover altogether—and then get a deer up and moving.

Most deer are shot under a Plan B—in thick cover or small, out-of-the-way spots: places that nobody else wants—or even thinks—to hunt. Put thick, small and out-of-the-way together, and you may have a deer hunting micro-hotspot for a long time.

Lunch time is hunting time for these farmland deer hunters. When everyone else is out of the woods, it's time to conduct some small, mini-pushes through known hiding cover. The keys: knowing well-used deer escape routes, being willing to root about in the thick of things with the deer, using the wind to your advantage ... and doing it often enough that sooner or later one of your plans will work just so!

The best time to do this is at the noon hour when other hunters are in town or at their trucks eating lunch—or during the afternoon when everyone else is at home or in a bar watching the Badger or Hawkeye or Packer or Bears football game. We're good neighbors and good stewards of the land we hunt, but not so generous as to want to put deer in the laps of every hunter in the township. So we love these times when we are alone in the woods, not a shot ringing from anywhere, imagining we are the only guys who know that deer season is open.

And for a few magical hours in the warmth of a November day, for all intents and purposes, that is true.

I once shot a very good doe this way—yes, I'd call her a Big Doe—at high noon.

I had been waiting for an hour at the end of the woodlot, as my father meandered through. She trotted up in the crunchy leaves—I could hear her coming for a full minute, stopping and

starting many times as she tested the wind, which was blowing at crosslots to us, my heart beating faster and louder in my ears with each scuffling of leaves—before she came to a statuesque pose 40 yards away across the draw.

I drew a bead carefully and shot, and as she whirled to run I saw the slug hole in her side. Browntown's noon whistle blew as I searched for her, and I found her under a hazelnut tree, one of the few left in this county, a half hour later. Her fat had sealed the wound, which explained the lack of a blood trail.

Our best buck ever came from one of these sneaking mini-pushes, an 8-pointer my father shot. It happened like this.

The lunch bunch has not yet returned to the neighboring woodlands, and not a deer is moving. We are getting quite sleepy too, my father and I, in the early afternoon sun after some morning fog and rain, and haven't seen much of anything.

Let's do a little sneak, I say, and he agrees, maybe hoping I will call it quits after I make my loop so that we can go home to rest.

So I give him a half hour to get into position in a steep, wooded gully that seems to collect deer moving through the south end of a certain sidehill wood-lot. I sneak around to the north end and then start hunting my way through the oak forest, quietly, looking hard for deer but more just enjoying the day. At one of my pauses, a twig snaps far ahead of me. I contemplate it briefly, then move on.

Perhaps 100 yards from my father, I hear another twig snap, so I stop again. One minute passes, two, then three. Just as I move to take another step, one shot from ahead cracks the silence. I wait, heart pounding and shotgun at-the-ready, for something to come sneaking back through. Then I can't wait any longer so I stalk quickly to where Dad should be.

He is not there, but some scuff marks in the leaves across the gully from where he should have been tell some more of the story. A deer was sneaking ahead of me, and Dad was in the perfect spot to intercept the skulking animal. So I walk out of the timber and there is Dad, standing over a buck. The deer died after crossing an alfalfa patch, heading into a marsh, one shot through the heart.

One antler sweeps above the grass there, and I know this is no ordinary buck as I quick-step over, Dad noticing me now and saying, a big smile on his face, come down here and do your work. Which means—come here and field dress this deer for me, whippersnapper.

We hug—briefly but with true happiness at our success—and then I go to work.

Of course, hearing about the successes like this, one might believe that shooting a deer here is easy. It's not. Remember—you are hearing the select stories of over a quarter century of hunting. We get a deer most years but not every year, certainly not a buck every year.

First of all, you have to be close enough to shoot. Although there is a farm over every other hill, the hills are big and the country is still pretty big and you have to be within 50 yards to have a decent chance of dropping a deer with a slug-loaded shotgun. You see many deer just outside that 75-yard range where sending a slug—even with all of today's technology behind it as well as in the firearm that's propelling it—means sending a little prayer as well.

The land rolls and folds upon itself. A deer can disappear in the middle of a field just when you're ready to pull the trigger, and then he'll emerge a hundred yards later, out of range. Or he might be out there a ways and disappear, then suddenly emerge almost in your lap. Rifled slugs and muzzleloaders are legal during the firearms season.

> *In the end, just being out there— persistence—is the key to much of our hunting success.*

Missing is a common occurrence in shotgun-and-slug country. I have taken unscientific polls of other hunters, landowners, game wardens and check-station biologists, asking—of every shot or volley of shots you hear, how many produce a deer for a hunter? 50 percent is the high end of what I hear, 25 percent the low end, with 33 percent being the most common answer and the one I tend to believe.

Yes, we too miss deer. And sometimes these misses are spectacular. Like the year when, at noon (of course) on the second day I was doing a small sneak-push when a deer came trotting through the grass and brambles toward me as I worked through a forgotten corner of cover—mostly just grass and black raspberry tangles. Probably rousted by my father, the young buck wasn't looking where he was going, and I hunkered behind a lone hickory tree and let him come. He stopped at 15 yards, smelling something out of place as the wind swirled and he caught my scent, and I shot. He took off, and I didn't even shoot again, expecting him to drop at any moment. He didn't.

I watched him trot across a quarter mile of cut corn, stopping to look back once or twice, the sun glinting off his small but nice little rack. If deer can think such things, he was surely thanking his lucky stars for the inept shooting of that hunter—me.

One story on missing is enough.

In the end, just being out there—persistence—is the key to much of our hunting success. That's why we pack in thermoses and food, even though it would only be a mile or so, sometimes less, of walking to the vehicles. Why waste good hunting time trudging out to get something to eat when you can do it sitting on your stool or backed up against a fencepost or cottonwood tree or hay bale, as you watch a field?

We got a doe one year in such a fashion.

Dad and I are leaning against a tree in a fencerow; the season is quite old and we haven't even seen a deer yet today. We are eating sandwiches when a deer hops into our field, 50 yards down the fenceline, looks at us, and starts trotting across the meadow and toward the woods. Sandwiches and coffee cups flying, we grab our guns and I duck aside so we can both shoot and one of us hits the deer—it doesn't matter who to us—as the animal reaches the woods.

We walk over and find her there on her side. We don't really seem to mind the interruption to our lunch, which I retrieve, and we finish it there beside her before dressing her out.

A haybale on the timber's edge to break up your silhouette, a good seat, a thermos of coffee, sustenance in the form of sandwiches and snacks, a spread of good woodlots, creekbottom and farm fields in front of you: In the middle of a long wait for a Cadiz Township buck or doe.

How many times have you heard about the littlest deer a hunting party ever took? You won't hear it admitted out loud, ever, but I'm going to tell you about ours, right here. I call it "The Lost Mitten Buck." He was a fawn-of-the-year.

It's the third day of the season, cold and windy because a snowstorm blew through on days one and two, and now arctic high pressure is whistling in. We haven't had much luck yet, the weather being so bad every day, and we can only stay on stand an hour or so after dawn, before numbing to the point of not being able to talk or even feel our fingers or toes. The whipping, northwesterly wind saps away every bit of heat our bodies can produce.

To warm up, I make a big swing through a CRP field—the woods seem empty, and maybe some deer are hiding in the gullies out here, out of the wind and collecting some warming sun. Mostly I am trying to generate some heat, as Dad bravely volunteers to stand watch in the valley bottom below in case I jump something on four legs and with hooves and a snowy-white tail.

After my roundabout, weaving circuit of about a mile total, circulation restored, I finally reach Dad and notice I have lost a glove—a good one,

part of my favorite hunting pair. Of course it is my right glove that is missing. I take it off for quick-shooting in such situations, and some bush or bramble must have snaked it from my coat pocket.

So back I go, retracing my steps in the new snow and looking for the red glove. In one particular gully, as I near a raspberry patch I had walked through, a rustling alerts me. Rabbit, I think at first, but out pops a deer practically at my feet! Reacting instinctively, I swing and shoot one, two, three times before he scurries around a rock outcropping and out of sight. The only deer tracks around the thicket lead out—he let me walk right by him the first time, earlier this morning.

I follow, dutifully, and soon come upon a nubbin buck, dead below a plum bush. He is warm to the touch, at the end of the tracks I am following. Yes, he is mine. My slug caught him below the ear, severing an artery.

He was not big, but he sure tasted good that winter.

I have shot one other deer coming out of its bed, and this one was more recent. It happened on a very warm, almost too-warm, October-like day when I was trying to walk up some action for us late in the season.

There is a certain little brush patch on a southwest-facing sidehill. The area used to be a pasture, but has since grown over with crabapple, plum brush, raspberry bushes and Russian olive, among a scattering of big old white oaks. Nobody ever hunts this acre-or-so patch of scrub and brush. But deer like it here, and we know it.

Dad waits to the east over the hill, so I sneak way up on the ridge and around, wind in my face, come down through fallow pastures, and then wade into the mostly-waist-high cover. The trick in this brush patch is to be positioned correctly on the sidehill so that when a deer jumps up you can get a shot or, better yet, be where your presence will cause the deer to swing away from you and toward whoever is waiting at the end of the fenceline that leads over the hill. The trouble is, you never know exactly where the deer will be lying, if there's one there at all that day.

A trophy's value lies in the feelings of its beholder, in your love of the countryside you took it from, and in the effort, time and commitment it took to get it. Throw in a golden, warm November day and the memory will last a lifetime.

Hunting the patch is also a trick because you have to be close enough to make the deer move, or they will just let you pass by.

So I must be coming through at just the right spot, shotgun above my head as I push through a particularly thick tangle, because suddenly I hear a rustling just ahead and it sounds bigger than a rabbit. It's a deer, getting up and starting its first bound as I bring the shotgun down to my shoulder. Hooves hit the ground as the gun's butt hits my shoulder and I look through the scope and swing as the deer takes off on its second bound—I remember the sound of the "thump" as hooves strike turf—and her silhouette fills the glass as I swing through and then it is over.

> *Hooves hit the ground as the gun's butt hits my shoulder and I look through the scope and swing as the deer takes off on its second bound ...*

The shot broke her back, and I have to bull my way over and then look the other way as I deliver a finisher, holding back a tear and wishing I hadn't been so lucky on this warm November day. I sit beside the doe for awhile, and I can see her last bed under a crabapple tree 20 feet away. The sun is warm on us, the sky blue above, and the earth smells good.

There are so many stories to tell.

I could talk about my dad's first buck—yes his first—shot in a driving rainstorm as the deer walked head-down across a still-green alfalfa field. I watched the whole drama from my stand on a hillside fenceline—seeing the 8-pointer trudging head-down in the rain and then rear up and fall over, shot smack through both shoulders. I reached the deer before Dad who, even way back then, didn't move very fast. We laughed together and I hugged him in the rain, knocking his glasses askew but they were fogged up anyway. As I dressed the buck, we talked of the years Dad had hunted for that moment—huffing up Puffinrath's hill back at Muscoda way back in the '50s—and how it was good and special to be together for it now.

I'd try to paint you a picture of my mother, wrapped up in a sweater against the cold, coming out at night as we pull into the driveway, to see what, if anything, we had brought home.

Big old cottonwood tree. Hunting log records show that 6 deer have been shot from underneath or within a few yards of this tree, 6 more within a hundred yards, 7 more within 200 yards, and more beyond that on the rest of the farm.

I might tell you about sitting on stand the autumns before my first, second and third sons were born, thinking about bringing them to this place one day—to home, to deer country—to hunt.

I'd spin some yarns about my Uncle Alvin, from the years we hunted with him by Calamine. One season he had accidentally bought 16-gauge slugs instead of 20s, and talked his friend into driving all the way back into Platteville or Darlington on Opening Morning to buy him the right slugs while he hunted with the friend's gun. Or the year, after his heart surgery, when he awoke at 7:30 a.m. Opening Day, cooked and ate breakfast, drove to Calamine, walked into a tiny patch of woods, had another group of hunters push a buck to him (which he shot) and then drag the deer up the hill to his old Galaxy 500

Snapshots of some modern day does and bucks from the hills, woods and fields of Green County's Cadiz Township. The hunters have put on years, but the land still produces deer, and the hunting is still an adventure.

where they strapped it across the trunk. He was home by 10:00 a.m.

I could tell you the details about every deer we ever have shot, or missed, because it's all there, recorded in my collection of hunting log-books.

Yes, there are so many stories to tell—of course of deer shot, but also of deer that outsmarted us, to live and breed and make more deer like them.

But deer camp, and deer camp at home like deer camp anywhere, is also about family, not just hunting. So I would tell you more about that—about standing arm-in-arm with my brother Larry and brother-in-law Mark, across a field from my brother Chuck, doing a

dance-line routine and singing "hit me with your best shot," from a popular song for that time so long ago. Chuck had missed several deer that year, and this was our way of rubbing it in.

And I'd tell you to etch moments like that on your mind forever, when the worries of the world are carried away on the wind and you are standing there with people you love, in a field back in the middle of nowhere, laughing and not really caring if every deer in the township runs off, and seeing your brother across the way laughing even from this far away, even though he's maybe a little mad at you for ruining his hunt.

And I'd say don't let time let the memories fade, but think about them often and tell them to your children and then make the commitment to teach them or someone else how to hunt too—how to do something that matters with people that matter, in country you love.

And I'd tell you more about the country—about what Cadiz Township oak woods smell like in the rain, or even just the damp of melting frost. I'd try to describe November's light there—first the way a sunrise comes up pink against the clouds but it's still night if you look west, with the lights of Browntown still twin-

kling across the highway, maybe even some early holiday lights up already; or else late afternoon, when the orange sun rakes across the hills, adding depth and texture and a warm glow to everything. I'd even tell you how I love the clouds coming on, iron-gray and low, pulling in a November storm.

And I'd try to describe the quiet then in the late afternoon, maybe standing down on the banks of Skinner Creek as it snakes its way toward the Pecatonica, hearing the swish of the dark water's slow current on the outside of a bend. If you listen closely, you might hear kids voices—the voices of my brothers and I, when we lived in Browntown, fishing the creek for bullheads and suckers and maybe even a smallmouth now and again—still echoing here from summer afternoons decades ago.

And I'd talk about the land as a whole—a place not wild, but a place with some wild corners and pockets of seclusion, a land of crop fields and haymeadows and woods and hills and creekbottoms and marsh grass—made special by the deer that live there and by the chance to be there, if for only a few days a year, hunting.

Finally, I'd tell you about the special people that have let us hunt here all these years, about Walter and Laura. I'd tell you about leap-

Dawn over the corn stubble, meadows, swales, creekbottoms, pastures, fencelines and woodlots.

The farms—and the people who own them—are the land's main stewards and gatekeepers. But to build real, lasting friendships is what's most important of all: getting to know good people who work the land, and who probably even love it a little more than even you do.

ing up their back porch sweating on a mosquito-filled morning in mid-September, having dragged up the 5-point buck I had killed with a bow down behind their barns at dawn, and hooking up the tractor with Walt to pull the deer the final hundred yards because I was bushed and the buck weighed more than I did. I think Walt felt good to be a part of the hunt. I'd reminisce about saying hello to Laura at 5:30 on an Opening Morning, hugging and then visiting in whispers (I don't know why, we didn't want to scare any deer I guess) before going hunting. And I'd tell you about sitting on the porch with them on a summer's evening, visiting and watching the goldfinches (wild canaries, Laura called them) and just liking each others company.

And I'd talk about Wallace and Aileen, who still own the abutting farm where we do all our hunting now that that Walter and Laura have left their beloved farm of so many years. I'd try to describe the smiles of our "new" friends who have been so for a long time now. And I'd tell about the happiness they show for us when we drive up to their back door to show off a deer we got, and how good it is to know people like this, and that good people like this still exist in this day and age.

When I think of my last moments on earth, I wonder what images will pass through my mind. Certainly the people I love—wife, children, father and mother, brothers and sister, good friends. And I think I'll also go deer hunting, if only for a few fleeting moments.

It'll go something like this. I'm hunting with my father, in the golden sunset of a clear November day, the wind lying low and the sun poking through a cloud bank and the horizon, raking across the oak woods and hayfields and creekbottoms, glowing orange on the land.

We'll be watching the corn stubble together, our backs against a big old hickory tree, and a buck will be feeding out there—a buck that rep-resents the deer I've taken life from so many times in my life, even if I don't shoot another until I reach that moment.

But we won't have guns, nor will we care. We'll watch the buck a while, drifting and feeding slowly and silently across the corn stubble as we talk about good times and bad and what really mattered in life and how we loved to hunt together and how it will be good to be together again.

And then the buck will fade into the oak timber across the way as I too go away—somewhere that I don't know, to be with those I love, and once again visit the places I loved, the place I am imagining now—leaving a part of me with the buck to roam the land. And I will feel good.